D0060815

Guide to the
Etruscan and Roman Worlds
at the
University of Pennsylvania Museum
of Archaeology and Anthropology

WITHDRAWN BY THE
UNIVERSITY OF MICHIGAN LIBRARY

Frontispiece. *Terracotta antefix with female head from Caere (Cerveteri), Italy; 4th century BC. H. 26.5 cm. MS 1801.*

Guide to the
Etruscan and Roman Worlds
at the
University of Pennsylvania Museum
of Archaeology and Anthropology

Donald White, Ann Blair Brownlee,
Irene Bald Romano, and Jean MacIntosh Turfa

Edited by Lee Horne

University of Pennsylvania Museum of Archaeology and Anthropology

Copyright © 2002 by
University of Pennsylvania Museum of Archaeology and Anthropology
3260 South Street
Philadelphia, Pennsylvania 19104

All Rights Reserved

First Edition

Library of Congress Cataloging-in-Publication Data

    University of Pennsylvania. Museum of Archaeology
    and Anthropology.
        Guide to the Etruscan and Roman worlds at the
    University of Pennsylvania Museum of Archaeology
    and Anthropology / Donald White ... [et al.] ; edited
    by Lee Horne.
        p. cm.
    Includes bibliographical references and index.
    ISBN 1-931707-37-5 (alk. paper)
    ISBN 1-931707-38-3 (pbk. : alk. paper)
        1. Etruscans--Antiquities--Catalogs. 2. Romans--
    Antiquities--Catalogs. 3. Italy--Antiquities--Catalogs.
    4. Classical antiquities--Pennsylvania--Philadelphia--
    Catalogs. 5. University of Pensylvania. Museum of
    Archaeology and Anthropology--Catalogs. I. White,
    Donald, 1935- II. Horne, Lee. III. Title.
    DG12.3.P48 U55 2002
    016.938--dc21
                         2002008805

The bird motif used throughout this guide was taken from the cup shown in illustration 15.

Printed in the United States of America on acid-free paper.

To Josie, whose wit, determination, and resourcefulness have fired this enterprise ab ovo usque ad mala.

Contents

Illustrations

Preface and Acknowledgments

In a great research institution where staff resources and time must be divided among field work, research, teaching, and exhibition, the opportunity to renovate an entire suite of galleries does not knock all that often. Indeed, the last time the Museum's Roman gallery was renewed was in the 1950s when the Museum was half as old as it is today. And not since the 1920s has the Etruscan collection been displayed with anything approaching the completeness of the current exhibition. The Mediterranean Section is therefore pleased to inaugurate Worlds Intertwined: Etruscans, Greeks, and Romans, with three new galleries—An Introduction to the Classical World, The Etruscan World, and The Roman World. This guide accompanies these new exhibitions and is a companion guide to *The Ancient Greek World* (1995) which accompanies the Greek World Gallery.

Because one of the central missions of the Museum is to inform the public, we have conceived of these exhibitions as a way to illuminate ancient societies by explaining and contextualizing the way objects were created and used. This conception underlies the decision to focus and structure these galleries on a few key overarching themes: everyday life, politics and war, economy and trade, religion, and death and burial. These are supplemented by more specialized displays that concentrate on the particular strengths of the collection.

The principal personnel responsible for the planning and the intellectual content of these galleries are Dr. Ann Blair Brownlee, Dr. Irene Bald Romano, and Dr. Donald White, along with the consulting scholar for the Etruscan gallery, Dr. Jean MacIntosh Turfa. We are deeply indebted to Museum Director Dr. Jeremy A. Sabloff, Deputy Director for Operations Dr. Gerald Margolis, and the Museum's Board of Overseers for their encouragement to undertake this project. We would like to express our heartfelt thanks to the Advisory Committee for the Etruscan and Roman Exhibition Project, headed by Josephine Hueber, for the hard work of guiding us safely through the difficult waters of raising the funds needed to bring to fruition the exhibitions, programming, and publications encompassed by this project.

We are thankful to our many supporters, especially The National Endowment for the Arts, the Institute of Museum and Library Services, the Commonwealth of Pennsylvania, the William B. Dietrich Foundation, the Samuel H. Kress Foundation, and many other foundations, corporations, and individuals who gave generously. Especially gratifying has been the support of the Italian-American community in the Philadelphia area who raised the funds for the Roman World Gallery, named in honor of a distinguished son of Italy and citizen of Philadelphia, Andrew N. Farnese, Esq. We are also proud to have named the Etruscan World Gallery in honor of Kyle M. Phillips, Jr. (1934–1988), a noted American archaeologist who excavated the important Etruscan site of Murlo.

Many scholars, colleagues, and students contributed their expertise and advice on individual objects or groups of objects, and to all of these we are grateful: Demi Andrianou, Donald Bailey, Robert Baines, Marshall Becker, Cecilia Beer, Dietrich Berges, Philip P. Betancourt, Pia Guldager Bilde, Claudio Bizzarri, Larissa Bonfante, Giovanni Colonna, Richard De Puma, Keith De-Vries, Ingrid Edlund-Berry, Jane DeRose Evans, Stuart Fleming, Harriet Flower, Heide Frielinghaus, Francoise Gaultier, Andrew Goldman, Nancy de Grummond, Erika Harnett, Barbara Hayden, Norman Herz, Catherine Johns, Iefke van Kampen, Elfriede Knauer, Eric Kondratieff, Valentina Livi, Naomi Miller, Mette Moltesen, Helen Nagy, Andrew Oliver, Barbara Presseisen, Cynthia Reed, Ellen Reeder, David Gilman Romano, Chris Rorres, Brent Shaw, Lynn Smith, Allaire Brisbane Stallsmith, Roger Thompson, Karen Vellucci, P. Gregory Warden, and Nancy Winter.

Many individuals in every department of the Museum have assisted with the publication of this guide. We offer our whole-hearted thanks to all. Gillian Wakely, Associate Director for Programs, kept us always aware of our audience. Conservation of the objects was carried out by the Museum's Conservation Laboratory headed by Virginia Greene, with the assistance of Julie Lawson, Lynn Grant, and freelance conservator Tamsen Fuller. Photography of the objects was undertaken by Francine Sarin and Jennifer Chiappardi of the Museum's Photography Studio. Alessandro Pezzati, Archivist, and Charles S. Kline, Photo Archivist, provided archival information and tracked down additional photographs. Unless otherwise noted, all illustrations are courtesy of the University of Pennsylvania Museum Archives.

Dr. Lee Horne, with the assistance of Raymond Rorke, edited the exhibition texts and the text of this guide. Lynn Makowsky, Keeper of the Mediterranean Section, and Naomi Pitamber were indispensable in managing the object movement and record keeping. Production and publication of the guide lay in the competent hands of Walda Metcalf, Director of Publications. Jennifer Quick, Senior Editor in Publications, designed the guide with a skilled eye and hand. To all who participated in this project we would like to extend our deepest appreciation.

1

The Etruscan and Roman Collections of the University of Pennsylvania Museum of Archaeology and Anthropology

The collections of the Mediterranean Section of the University of Pennsylvania Museum of Archaeology and Anthropology comprise approximately 30,000 objects of Greek, Etruscan, Roman, Cypriot, and Bronze Age Aegean origins, as well as small numbers of objects from related culture areas. The majority of these objects were acquired before World War I, when the laws governing the export of antiquities made it possible.

The classical world and the acquisition of objects from classical lands, especially excavated archaeological material, was a primary interest of the Museum at its founding in 1887 and in its formative years. This was a reflection not only of the specific goals of the University Museum, but also of a general intense interest in classical antiquity in the late 19th and early 20th century in America. This interest was fostered by an educational system that emphasized classical literature and languages, and it was fueled in the 1870s by a fascination with Heinrich Schliemann's search for Homer's Troy.

The encouragement and financial support of luminaries of Philadelphia society who supported the Museum and sat on its Board—Lucy Wharton

Drexel, Phoebe A. Hearst, and John Wanamaker—made possible many of the important early acquisitions of the Mediterranean Section. These activities were guided by Sara Yorke Stevenson, who became Curator of the Mediterranean Section of the Museum in 1894. In 1895 the Museum made an arrangement with Arthur L. Frothingham, Jr., a professor at Princeton University and Associate Director of the American School in Rome (later the American Academy in Rome), to serve as an agent for the Museum in locating and purchasing antiquities and plaster casts suitable for the Museum's classical collections. Frothingham's purchases were to shape the Etruscan and Roman collections immeasurably.

THE ETRUSCAN COLLECTIONS

Arthur Frothingham played a critical role in the formation of the Museum's Etruscan collections, and while many of the objects, such as the important series of architectural terracottas from Caere (Cerveteri) and Tarquinia, were purchased from dealers in Rome, Frothingham also employed Italian excavators to conduct excava-

1. The Phoebe A. Hearst Collection, which includes most of the Etruscan material, as it was set up when the Museum opened in 1899.

tions and provide documentation for the finds. One particular excavator, Francesco Mancinelli Scotti, excavated tombs at the important Etruscan city of Vulci and the Faliscan town of Narce. A careful excavator by contemporary standards, he provided Frothingham with entire tomb groups—groups of objects from the same tomb—as well as documentation—plans, drawings, photographs, and lists of tomb contents. The young Museum, acquiring objects to fill the new building then under construction, was articulating a collecting policy whereby it would be less interested in individual objects and more concerned with acquiring whole groups of objects covering a large chronological range which had come from scientific exploration and which would be accompanied by care-

fully and scientifically gathered documentation. The new Etruscan collection, with its complete and well-documented tomb groups, was a perfect example of the Museum's mission.

A number of the Etruscan objects, particularly their black-fired *bucchero* pottery and small bronzes, but also the cinerary urn of Arnth Remzna, came from the collection of Robert H. Coleman. The entire collection was purchased by the Museum at auction, in February of 1897, with funds provided by Phoebe Hearst. Coleman, heir to an ironworks empire in Lebanon County, Pennsylvania, was one of the wealthiest men in America in the late 1880s until his bankruptcy soon after forced him to sell off his assets. When he formed his collection, it was probably with the assistance of an agent in Florence, James

2. The contents of the Museum's Tuscania tomb as shown in a photograph of ca. 1896.

Jackson Jarves. Jarves, whose father was the founder of the Boston and Sandwich Glass Company, was a well-known figure in Florence and served as American vice-consul from 1880 to 1882.

Phoebe Hearst was one of the most generous donors to the Mediterranean Section in the early years of the Museum. Funds for the Museum's sponsorship of Frothingham's work came largely from her. Six late Etruscan sarcophagi from Città Musarna, which arrived at the Museum in late 1900, were among the last of her gifts for the Mediterranean Section collections.

Apart from the Etruscan vases that came to the Museum through the Philadelphia Museum of Art loan of the early 1930s, there was no significant addition of Etruscan material until 1968, when the Museum purchased some thirty objects from the Hercle Excavation Company in Rome. A quasi-governmental organization, the Hercle company had been formed to excavate and legally export finds.

The Museum's collection comes from excavations at the necropolis at Vulci, the so-called *zona dell Osteria*.

The Museum continues its archaeological interest in Etruria. Since 1997 it has been collaborating with Southern Methodist University to excavate the Etruscan site of Poggio Colla in the Mugello Valley north of Florence.

THE ROMAN COLLECTIONS

While a clear line is drawn today between genuine ancient artifacts and replicas in museum displays, that line was not so firmly drawn for museum audiences of the late 19th and early 20th centuries. When the Museum opened in 1899, the displays in the Pepper Hall on the second floor, the core of the classical galleries, were a creative combination of cast replicas and archaeological collections acquired in Italy. Among the replicas in this early 1900s display that still form

3. Pepper Hall of the Museum, ca. 1906. By 1906 casts of famous sculptural works of classical antiquity, like the Venus de Milo and the Victory of Samothrace, had been added to the collections. They were put on display in an eclectic arrangement of replicas and artifacts, including some of the marble sculptures from the Sanctuary of Diana at Lake Nemi.

an important part of the collection are over 400 bronzes, ranging from objects of everyday life to life-size statues, which had been cast from molds taken from original artifacts excavated from Pompeii and Herculaneum. These were manufactured in the Naples workshop of J. Chiurazzi and Son at the end of the 19th century. Philadelphia philanthropist and department store magnate John Wanamaker purchased them for the Museum in 1904.

In addition to the Etruscan collections, one of Arthur Frothingham's greatest acquisitions for the Museum was a group of 45 marble sculptures from the Sanctuary of Diana Nemorensis on the shores of Lake Nemi, south of Rome. With the permission of the land owner, Prince Filippo Orsini, the site had been explored in 1895 by

Lord Savile, the British ambassador in Rome, and by a group of Roman art dealers from 1886 to 1888. By 1896 pieces from Nemi were beginning to be offered on the art market. The Museum, through its emissary Frothingham, vied with the newly founded Ny Carlsberg Glyptotek in Copenhagen, through its agent in Rome Wolfgang Helbig, to purchase the rich trove of marble sculptures from the site. While the Glyptotek in Copenhagen won the larger Imperial portrait statues from Nemi, the Museum was able to purchase in 1896 important Republican period votive statuettes and marble vessels that are unique in the United States. In 2001 the Museum reestablished its connections with Nemi and the Ny Carlsberg Glyptotek in a collaborative project

4. John Wanamaker (1838–1922). Wanamaker was a prominent Philadelphia businessman and a member and vice-president of the Board of Managers of the University of Pennsylvania Museum from 1896 to 1922.

with the Nordic Institutes in Rome to excavate at a Roman villa site on the shores of Lake Nemi, within Diana's sacred grove.

Many Roman objects in the Mediterranean Section represent individual purchases or gifts, with and without proveniences. Others came as collections. Several, like that from Lake Nemi, stand out as important for their size, quality, and uniqueness. Among these early acquisitions was the collection of engraved gems and cameos of Maxwell Sommerville. Sommerville was one of the more eccentric individuals in the Museum's history, vice-president of the Museum from 1894 to 1904,

Professor and Curator of Glyptology. He was a partner in a Philadelphia publishing firm, a self-educated student of archaeology, and an avid collector of ancient gems. In 1899 he deeded his collection, which numbered some 3,400 pieces, to the Museum. The collection is recognized today as an eclectic one,

5. Marble sculptures from the Sanctuary of Diana in a storage room in Italy, ca. 1895. All of these pieces were purchased by the University of Pennsylvania Museum, except the large head of Diana to the far right which went to Copenhagen.

6. Portrait of Maxwell Sommerville (1829–1904) in an oil painting by Stephen J. Ferris, 1893. The portrait is in the collections of the University of Pennsylvania Museum.

composed of 17th, 18th, and 19th century Classicizing gems, as well as approximately 600 ancient gems.

The collection of Hermann V. Hilprecht of over 300 classical bronzes, the majority votive figurines, was accessioned by the Museum in 1948, though on loan since 1934. Hilprecht (1859–1925) was for many years Professor of Assyriology at the University of Pennsylvania, Curator of the Babylonian and General Semitic Section of the Museum from 1888–1910, and an eminent Mesopotamian scholar. The majority of these classical bronzes, given to the Museum by Hilprecht's niece after his death, were collected by him between 1893 and 1909 in the bazaars of Istanbul. Additional pieces were collected during his travels to other parts of the Ottoman Empire. Some of Italic origin were purchased from dealers in Italy. For each piece Hilprecht kept meticulous records of its purchase, provenience, and description. In 1895 Hilprecht also purchased for the Museum's collections two unusual Roman lead coffins made in the region of Phoenician Tyre in the late 2nd–early 3rd centuries AD. These he bought in a less exotic city—Newark, New Jersey—from an Armenian dealer, Daniel Noorian, who was Hilprecht's interpreter at Nippur, Iraq.

The Museum's substantial collection of Roman coins, numbering in the thousands, was5 acquired from various sources. The major gift of Roman coins, however, was given by Robert C. H. Brock (1861–1906) around 1898–99. Brock was a Philadelphia lawyer, a colonel in the National Guard, and vice-president of the Museum's Board from 1898 to 1902. Having an ongoing interest in building up the Museum's coin collections, Brock also purchased a large group of Islamic and Asian coins for the Museum.

In addition to purchasing coins, the Museum has important numismatic collections from archaeological excavations. The Egyptian Section excavations at Memphis (Mit-rahinah) from 1915 to 1923 and at Meydum in 1929 to 1932 provided large numbers of Roman coins, including a coin hoard of around 2,300 specimens dating to the 4th–5th centuries AD that was found in a single jar at Meydum. The Near Eastern Section's excavations between 1921 and 1933 at Beth Shean also yielded 85 coins, mostly of Late Roman date. More recently, the

7. Hermann Hilprecht (1859–1925). Hilprecht's large collection of classical bronzes was donated to the Museum in 1948.

Museum acquired a small group of Roman coins from the 1960s excavations of T. A. Carter at Leptis Magna.

One of the last major Roman archaeological collections acquired by the Mediterranean Section was the material from the site of Minturnae. Located on the west coast of Italy between Rome and Naples, Minturnae was excavated by the Museum under the direction of Jotham Johnson from 1931 to 1933. At the conclusion of Johnson's field work the Museum received a generous division of the finds, including eight marble sculptures, pottery, lamps, and important Italo-Etruscan architectural terracottas.

Few acquisitions have been added to the Roman collections since the 1950s. One important exception is a gift of Roman glass, mostly collected in the 19th century by William Sansom Vaux (1811–1882) and presented to the Museum in 1986 by his great-nephews George and Henry J. Vaux. The Vaux collection added in quality and num-

bers to the Museum's already distinguished collections of Roman glass acquired earlier. In 1916 Lydia Morris had given the Museum Roman glass that had been collected by her brother, John T. Morris. In 1913, other pieces had been purchased by the Museum from Vester & Company, and from 1921 to 1931 a large group of Roman glass in the Near Eastern Section had been excavated by the Museum in the cemeteries at Beth Shean.

The Museum's classical collections are augmented by objects on long-term loan that are displayed and published along with the Museum's own holdings. Lenders in this mutually beneficial arrangement include the Philadelphia Museum of Art, the Max von Oppenheim Foundation, the Department of Classics at Swarthmore College, the Department of Classical Studies and Ancient History at the University of Pennsylvania, and the Glencairn Museum in Bryn Athyn, Pennsylvania.

The heartland of Etruria in north central Italy, including sites mentioned in the text.

8 (opposite). View of the hilltop town of Orvieto. The ancient Etruscan city lies under the modern town.

Courtesy of E. R. Knauer.

2

The Etruscan World

Etruria, homeland of the Etruscans, lay in north-central Italy, between the Tiber and the Arno Rivers and across the Apennines to the mouth of the Po. Here rose the cities of Italy's earliest civilization.

Travel and transport in Iron Age Italy followed mountain ridges and navigable rivers and streams. Etruscan cities grew out of villages situated at crossroads or river fords along these routes. Port towns arose on the coast to serve the cities. Resources, such as timber and metal ores, and control of the shipping lanes of the Tyrrhenian Sea formed the basis of Etruscan wealth. At the peak of their power in the late 8th through 6th centuries BC, Etruscan cities colonized wide areas of Italy, extending eastward to the Adriatic coast and south to Pompeii in the Bay of Naples.

In the 1st century BC, after Rome conquered the whole of Italy, only the voices of unsympathetic Greek and Roman historians survived to tell of Etruria's former glory. Today, scholars have begun to read again the story of Etruria in her tombstones, houses, works of art, and even her very bones. Much of our evidence comes from cemeteries, and these burials provide a window into Etruscan society as well as into the life and identity of individual Etruscans.

THE EARLIEST ETRUSCANS

The ancestors of the Etruscans had lived for centuries by tending crops, herding animals, spinning and weaving cloth, crafting bronze, and preparing for war. During the 9th–8th centuries BC, life began to change. The introduction of iron technology and an influx of foreign traders began to stimulate social and political development as well as material culture. Hut villages would soon develop into the cities that are still famous, such as Florence, Pisa, Bologna, and many more now lost.

By the 7th century BC, Etruscan culture had entered its "Orientalizing" phase. Foreign influences from the Near East and Greece now permeated art and society. Traders from Greece, Phoenicia, and Syria came to Italy to exchange luxury goods for metals and ores, making Etruria wealthy in the process. Interaction stimulated not only art and technology, but also society and politics. By the mid-7th century BC, Etruria was rich and powerful.

9. TERRACOTTA BICONICAL URN AND COVER

Bisenzio, 8th century BC
H. with lid, 49.5 cm
MS 1598

Distinctive biconical urns, made of clay and baked in hearths, were used in homes as well as in the burials of the cremated dead. During the funeral ritual, bones were swept up from the pyre, pounded into small fragments, and wrapped in a cloth, perhaps fastened with the owner's *fibula* (a safety pin or brooch). A shallow bowl would be inverted over the top and tied on.

10. TERRACOTTA HUT URN

Said to have come from the area between Albano and Genzano, 8th century BC
H. 27.5 cm
MS 1601

A hut urn, in clay or metal, was an option for a special few. It symbolized the family's home or the home of its now-powerful ancestors.

11. BRONZE *FIBULA* WITH DISK FOOT AND AMBER BEAD

Bisenzio, 8th century BC
L. 12.9 cm
MS 1519

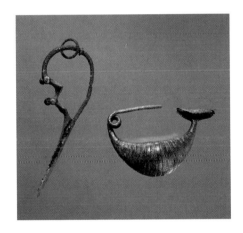

This *fibula* must have been a favorite belonging or an heirloom. It broke at its most-used points, the spring and the catch, and was painstakingly repaired with riveted plates of bronze. Note the coldwork designs engraved on the spiral catchplate. They match the incised decoration on urns and probably originated as colorful patterns woven into textiles.

12. BRONZE *FIBULAE*

Narce, 8th century BC
L. 10.6 cm
MS 1155

Narce, Tomb 18B. 8th century BC
L. 7.6 cm
MS 1137B

Bronze *fibula* of "drago" and "leech" types. Over time, *fibulae* developed to include different shapes for male or female use. The "drago" (dragon) shape is usually found in men's graves, the "leech" in women's graves.

13. BRONZE PENDANT

Narce, Tomb 23M, 7th century BC
L. 11.3 cm
MS 1044

This pendant is made of sheet bronze with repoussé decoration. The stag is a characteristic motif of this period.

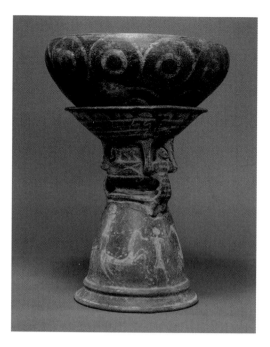

14. TERRACOTTA CONICAL STAND AND BOWL

Narce, Tomb 7, early 7th century BC
Diam. of bowl, 25.4 cm
MS 1221, MS 1222

This elaborate painted stand and bowl would have been used for private and civic banquets. The white-painted figures of men between profile horses are highly stylized yet full of motion. Two striped male figures, perhaps court acrobats, serve as supports for the bowl. During this period, a growing aristocratic class bred and drove horses as a sign of their wealth and power.

THE VILLANOVAN PERIOD

Etruria emerged from the Bronze Age with a distinctive culture already formed. We call this early period (9th–8th centuries BC) Villanovan, after a cemetery near Bologna. The people of the Villanovan period were a society of warrior-farmers living in small hut-villages. Their control of mines of metal ores and their expertise in metallurgy are hallmarks of this era.

The honored dead were cremated and buried in pits. Distinctive urns capped with a bowl or a warrior's helmet held the ashy bones. The family might deposit offerings of food in bowls or cups, and personal belongings, like a man's razor, tools, or weapons, or a woman's jewelry or spinning equipment.

During the 11th–10th centuries BC, most burial goods showed little differentiation in wealth, but by the 9th–8th centuries BC, an "elite" had emerged. As Etruria grew richer, her people car-ried objects of greater value into the afterlife. The first recognizable aristocrats received symbolic grave offerings: tokens of horse and chariot ownership, tributes of arms and armor, or jewelry made with imported Baltic amber.

THE ORIENTALIZING PERIOD

As Etruria grew in wealth and power, clusters of hut-villages coalesced into cities with rectangular, tile-roofed houses and sanctuaries. Municipal militias and governments oversaw the building of roads, aqueducts, marketplaces, and shrines. Such a large and stratified society called for greater organization, reflected in new systems of naming that added family or clan to the personal name.

Lavish narrative art was dependent on special materials from abroad (ivory, glass, stone for sculpture, painted pottery) and greatly influenced by Near

15. IMPASTO *KOTYLE*

Narce, Tomb I, 7th century BC
Diam. 8.4 cm
MS 2751

This cup combines a Greek shape—the deep cup called a *kotyle*—with Italian dark clay and is decorated with a stylized Geometric bird.

Eastern styles. This era has thus been called the "Orientalizing" period (ca. 730–580 BC). Customs, too, were affected by foreign contact, and Near Eastern modes of displaying kingly power were adopted by the chiefs of Italy.

Spirally grooved amphoras in coarse "impasto" clay, incised images of birds, painted patterns, as well as metal vases imitating the works of Phoenicia and Syria, are all characteristic of the new Orientalizing style. Vases of dark impasto fabric and native Italian shapes were gradually supplanted by wheel-made pottery painted in imitation of imported Greek wares.

Functional objects of bronze were decorated with monsters, animals or flowers from Near Eastern art. Stimulated by Greek imports, Etruscan artists began to develop figural and narrative art, with sculptures and paintings showing men or gods. The rendering of the human figure became increasingly natural. In imitation of the sophisticated products of the fabled East, artists created their own versions of monsters (sphinxes and griffins), palmettes, and exotic plants.

FALISCAN WARRIORS AND WEAVERS

The culture of the Faliscans, Etruria's nearest neighbors, was distinct from but closely related to that of the Etruscans. They spoke an Italic language unrelated to Etruscan, but used the Etruscan alphabet to write it. They shared the art and technology of the Etruscans and practiced similar funerary rites. As soon as foreign imports and technology appeared in the Etruscan cities, the Faliscans acquired them too.

From the 9th century on, Faliscan burial practices paralleled those of Etruria. The many famous "princely" or aristocratic burials of the late 8th and 7th centuries BC are renowned for their opulent displays of wealth and status. Their abundant contents reveal the gradual enrichment of Etruscan and Faliscan art with new materials, techniques, and images brought from the eastern Mediterranean. Warriors were buried with their armor, clothing, shaving equipment, vases for banqueting, and harnesses from their chariot teams. Their

16. In the late 19th century, the University of Pennsylvania Museum sponsored the excavation of a series of tombs at Narce, an important Faliscan town. These tombs, whose contents were carefully documented, provide a glimpse into the lives of Faliscan men, women, and children of the 7th century BC. The photograph shows most of the contents of Tomb 43.

wives were buried with riches and symbols of their own prowess as weavers that show they shared their husbands' high status and some of their authority.

Faliscan pottery, while influenced by Etruscan pottery, has its own distinctive style. Vases have twisted handles that turn into animal's heads, and forms and decoration are flamboyantly combined. Most retain the impasto fabric made from the coarse, dark-colored clays favored throughout prehistoric Italy. As in Etruria, craftsmen often made ceramic copies of the bronze conical stands used by rulers for banquet wine. The more economical material allowed large scale, extravagant forms.

17. BRONZE CRESTED HELMET
Narce, Tomb 43, end of 8th
century BC
H. 43 cm
MS 850

A commander's crested helmet allowed him to be seen from a distance by his skirmishers. This one is decorated with geometric patterns. It is one of two helmets buried with the warrior.

18. BRONZE CUIRASS

Narce, Tomb 43, end of 8th century BC
H. 41.4 cm
MS 851

This heavy bronze cuirass would have protected the warrior in hand-to-hand combat. Only the front section is preserved. Its geometric patterns match those on the crested helmet.

19. BRONZE LUNATE RAZOR

Narce, Tomb 43, end of 8th century BC
L. 10.8 cm
MS 853

Razor handles had an eyelet so they could be hung from a hook or pinned to a cloak. This one is cast with stylized, angular bird heads.

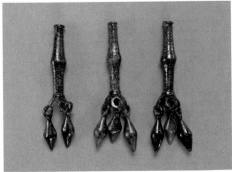

20. BRONZE PENDANTS

Narce, Tomb 19M, early 7th century BC
L. 8.4 cm
MS 787A–C

These hollow pendants, with three heavy, biconical bronze beads hanging from large eyelets, may have been weights for a woman's belt or scarf. They would have jingled as their wearer walked.

21. IMPASTO FOOTED BOWL

Narce, Tomb 19M, early 7th century BC
H. 25.5 cm
MS 761

This bowl has ornate openwork decoration depicting the "Master of Horses."

22. IMPASTO *KANTHAROS*

Narce, Tomb 1, mid 7th century BC
H. with handle 19.6 cm
MS 2734

The ram's head handles on the amphora are a hallmark of Faliscan potters.

DAILY LIFE IN ETRURIA

Most of our information about Etruscan life comes from images and personal belongings found in Etruscan tombs. Paintings on the walls of the larger tombs display funeral banquets, processions, and games that must have been adapted from the happier events in life—civic ceremonies, state dinners, weddings, and rituals of worship. Favorite personal belongings taken to the tomb show us what men and women wore and valued in life. Sometimes large tombs symbolize the deceased's home, which helps us understand what the house of a well-to-do Etruscan looked like.

We know very little about the majority of Etruscans—those who could not afford chamber tombs or burial gifts of non-perishable materials. Scenes of "average" people at work and play do exist, but most pictures portray only important persons and their families.

Men's Lives

During the 7th century BC, life changed drastically for most Etruscans and evolved into a complex schedule of daily, urban activities. More people now lived in cities, in houses instead of

23. GOLD TUBULAR EARRINGS
5th–4th centuries BC
Diam. 2.5 cm
MS 3344A, B

GOLD HORSESHOE-TYPE EARRING
4th century BC
L. 4.7 cm
MS 310

Tubular or bugle shaped earrings were easy to fasten: the narrower end was simply forced into the wider. Horseshoe-type earrings appear on the antefix in the frontispiece.

24. CARNELIAN SEAL
5th century BC
L. 1.9 cm
29-128-542

Carved in the distinctive Etruscan style called *a globolo*, this seal shows a charioteer driving a three-horse chariot (*triga*). Originally a war machine that used the third horse to carry armor, the *triga* was a racing chariot in Etruria, with the extra challenge of controlling the horse in traces. *Triga* races appear in the funeral games that are depicted on the walls of Etruscan tombs at Tarquinia and Chiusi.

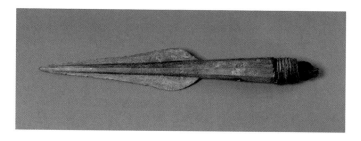

25. BRONZE SPEARPOINT
Bisenzio, 8th–7th centuries BC
L. without shaft, 24.8 cm
MS 1525

Part of the wooden shaft is preserved inside the bronze spear-point. The tip of the shaft has been carefully carved and hardened to a point to fit the cast spearpoint perfectly. A well-balanced spear can be thrown most accurately.

26. BRONZE JOCKEY-TYPE HELMET
4th century BC
H. 32 cm
MS 1606

This Etruscan helmet with cheek protectors was a design taken over from the Gauls during the 4th century BC and was later adopted by the Romans as well.

27. BRONZE BIT
7th century BC
L. 26.5 cm
MS 1637

Bronze was often preferred for ornamental horse harness, such as this bit of a type manufactured in Vetulonia. It was probably not for war or work, but a parade ornament: the cheek pieces are decorated with Phoenician palmettes.

28. ETRUSCO-CORINTHIAN
OLPE

Vulci, Tomb B, 6th century BC
H. 25.1 cm
MS 714

Rendered in imitation of Corinthian painting style is a line of Etruscan warriors wearing helmets and carrying round shields. Their identical armor and marching step suggest the militia of an Etruscan city and patterns of warfare like the "phalanx" that were learned from the Greeks.

huts, traveled on paved streets in chariots or carts, and worked in (or owned) factories and shops.

In the city, men of influence took charge of government and the military as well as their own businesses. Such a man's daily routine was organized around his home, probably in the way it was described by Romans of the 3rd–1st centuries BC. House plans illustrate this with a public reception area or *atrium* for business and guests and a more private domain for family use.

The Etruscan House

By the 6th century BC, many Etruscan villages had coalesced into towns, their huts replaced with rectangular houses of wood or mudbrick on stone foundations. Such houses might have an inner courtyard or hall open to the sky, room to work, simple plumbing, and wood paneling. Bedrooms and storage areas were in the back or upstairs.

29. *FOCOLARE* TRAY
Chiusi, 6th century BC
W. 51 cm
MS 1355–1363

Sixth-century tombs at Chiusi often held imitation sets of banquet utensils made in *bucchero* pottery instead of bronze or silver. These include miniature plates, bowls, and ladles placed inside a portable brazier.

This pattern evolved into the famous "atrium house" of Rome and Pompeii.

In comparison to modern houses, ancient Mediterranean houses seem bare, with very little furniture. In fact, Etruscans paid great attention to interior decorating. We know this from their tombs, decorated like paneled houses, and from rare finds of actual furniture. They furnished their houses with more utensils and furniture than did the Greeks, making the interiors attractive and comfortable. The Romans emulated them, as the houses of Pompeii attest. Greek aristocrats sought out Etruscan silver and bronze ware as the best that money could buy.

30. BRONZE TORCH HOLDER
4th century BC
H. 36.6 cm
MS 5697

Bronze torch holders were carried on long poles to light the tomb or to find one's way through dark city streets. Wedding processions were led by torchbearers.

Women's Lives

The home was a focus for Etruscan women as well as for men. In spite of changing times, women still spun and wove to clothe their families, as they had throughout the centuries. The new city life, however, meant managing a larger household and entertaining at public and private affairs. Women married young, probably as teenagers, and often bore many children. The affluent, however, found time for travel, hobbies, and even managing their own businesses. Inscriptions show that women could own or inherit real estate, and on occasion ran establishments such as fine pottery workshops.

Compared to their Greek counterparts, upper- and middle-class Etruscan women lived liberated lives. Many women drove or rode in their own chariots. They gave parties and banquets for their female friends. Much official entertaining revolved around married couples, however, with the wives reclining beside their husbands at banquets.

31. TERRACOTTA *PYXIS*

Narce, Tomb I, 7th century BC
H. 16.9 cm
MS 2732A, B

This painted box probably held a lady's jewelry, cosmetics, or medicines; it is supported by three "feet" wearing pointed shoes.

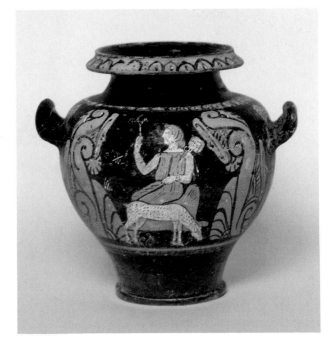

32. ETRUSCAN RED-FIGURED *STAMNOS*

4th century BC
H. 28.9 cm
MS 2520

This vase shows a fawn and a seated maenad who seems to mimic a woman spinning thread from fresh wool on her distaff. The goddess Menrva stands on the other side of the vase.

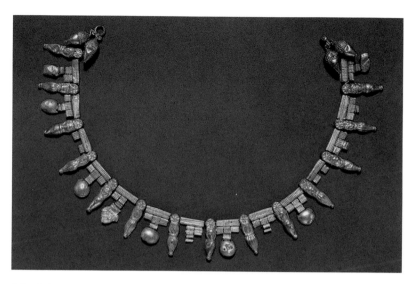

33. GOLD NECKLACE
4th century BC
L. 34.0 cm
MS 4021

Elaborate necklaces such as this were costly and fragile. This one includes hollow pendants in the shape of vases from which female heads emerge.

Jewelry

Gold jewelry, known since the 7th century BC from the so-called princely tombs, became increasingly common in the 6th century BC and later. Etruscan gold work, especially pieces decorated by the granulation technique, was a technological achievement of the Archaic period. Gold earrings were very popular and changed rapidly with the fashions. Goldsmiths also made false teeth attached to permanent teeth by gold bands.

Glass beads in blue, white and yellow, with "eye" patterns, were prized in Etruria from the late 8th century BC on. They were usually worn in necklaces. Expensive jewelry displayed a family's wealth and social status, setting nobles apart from the rest of the citizenry.

34. GOLD EARRINGS
6th century BC
Diam. 1.5 cm
MS 3345A–C

The "carpet-bag" (a baule) type earrings were made in opposite pairs for right and left ears. The earrings are decorated with granulation, and it is possible to tell that the craftsman was right-handed by the direction in which he twisted the wire ornaments. The bottom two are a pair.

THE ETRUSCAN LANGUAGE

The Etruscan language is not like Latin, Italian, or any of the other languages of Italy. These are Indo-European, as are most modern European languages, including English. Etruscan may instead represent a prehistoric language spoken in Italy before the invasions of the Italic tribes, including the Latins, sometime before the first millennium BC.

Knowledge of the Etruscan language was once considered "lost." It has not been spoken since the Roman Empire, and for long before that it was spoken only by priests. Yet contrary to popular belief, we can—and do—read and understand Etruscan. Our knowledge is constrained only by the limited nature of the surviving inscriptions: we have tomb markers and votive dedications, cryptic calendars and incantations, but no diaries or literature. Literary works on papyrus and linen have not survived.

The Etruscans were a highly literate people. Because their religious teachings were written and shared over many centuries, they have sometimes been called "people of the book." Many men and women, both aristocrats and artisans, could read and write, to judge from the inscribed objects that have been found. These "talking objects" seem to express magically the power that ancient peoples felt came from the ability to read and write. It was a power of which Etruscan men and women were justly proud.

35. NENFRO LINTEL
Orvieto, Crocifisso del Tufo necropolis, ca. 550 BC
L. 190 cm
MS 3200

The inscription on this lintel of volcanic stone (nenfro) runs from right to left, as do most Etruscan inscriptions, and records the name of the subscriber:

mi [ ] velthurus hulchenas kav

"I belong to Velthur Hulchenas. . . {son of Kav——}"

The subscriber's first name, Velthur, was a favorite choice for male Etruscans. His second name, Hulchenas, shows his family affiliation. The third, fragmentary name may have denoted his father's name.

36. TERRACOTTA URN AND LID

From a tomb in the territory of Chiusi, 2nd century BC
L. 34.8 cm
57-3-1A, B

Inscriptions were also used to identify cinerary urns such as this one, which bears a painted inscription, "θania:anainei:apiasa," which means Thania Apiasa, daughter of Anainei. The cremated remains of Thania Apiasa, who was also named for the goddess Thana, were placed in a mold-made terracotta urn decorated with a winged head of Medusa with foliage and ribbons. The lid shows a generic effigy of a reclining woman.

TECHNOLOGY AND COMMERCE

By the 9th century BC, Etruscans had mastered mining and the working of bronze and iron. During the Archaic and Classical periods (6th through 4th centuries BC), foreign trade stimulated new technologies: goldsmithing, glassmaking, mass production of terracotta tiles and urns, and monumental stone carving. Metal crafting and pottery continued to thrive.

Etruria's most distinctive products were sought throughout the Mediterranean world. Fine vases, metal utensils, arms and armor, wine, grain, and timber were exchanged for Baltic amber, Gaulish slaves, Athenian olive oil, Corinthian and Rhodian perfumes, or glass, faience, and ivories from Phoenicia, Syria, or Egypt.

Etruscan cities came to be known for their different specialties. Vulci, for example, produced wines, pottery, and fine metal goods for wide export. Orvieto (Volsinii) shipped raw products

37. *BUCCHERO* CHALICE

Vulci, Tomb 5, early 6th century BC
H. 15.3 cm
MS 560A

A *bucchero* version of the native vase shape, this chalice is enlivened by caryatids—female figurines serving as supports.

38. BUCCHERO KANTHAROS

Chiusi, 6th century BC
W. 24 cm
L-64-539

The plain *kantharos* shape is here given a scalloped rim and is ornamented with the "Mistress of the Animals" (once a Near Eastern fertility goddess) on the handles and sphinxes on the bowl.

39. ETRUSCO-CORINTHIAN *OINOCHOE*

Vulci (Pitigliano), Tomb 26, early
6th century BC
Attributed to the Bearded Sphinx Painter
H. with handle 27 cm
MS 642

The Bearded Sphinx Painter, who worked in Vulci, chose to imitate Corinthian wares.

from the Italian interior, along with fine manufactured goods including *bucchero* and gilded vases. Chiusi, farther north and inland than Vulci or Orvieto, developed a quaint style of its own in pottery, stonework, and metalwork. In the cemeteries of these and other Etruscan cities, we find the goods that were prized at home and abroad, the non-perishable tokens of a thriving long-distance trade.

Pottery

During the 7th century BC, Etruscans developed a distinctive shiny, solid black pottery today called *bucchero*. *Bucchero* pottery enjoyed wide popularity both at home and abroad. During the 6th century BC, they also created distinctive wares that imitated the imported pottery of Corinth and Athens. The impasto pottery characteristic of early Etruria continued to be made for everyday use.

Etrusco-Corinthian ware, developed in the late 7th century BC, combines elements from Corinthian pottery with native, Etruscan features. Often the style is so distinctive that it is possible to identify individual painters.

40. ETRUSCAN BLACK-FIGURED NECK-AMPHORA

6th century BC
Attributed to the Jerusalem Painter
H. 47.9 cm
L-29-47

This Etruscan neck-amphora shows how the black-figure technique was borrowed and adapted for Etruscan taste. The Etruscan artist relies entirely on the black silhouette to tell his story; there is little of the incised detail and none of the added color that characterize Corinthian and Attic black-figured wares.

On loan from the Philadelphia Museum of Art.

The black-figure technique of Archaic Athens was also an inspiration to Etruscan artists. Again, they often chose particular elements from Attic painting to imitate or enlarge on. They showed little regard for the ideal proportions and restraint of Greek artists, and often their scenes verged on the comic.

Metalworking

Greeks, Gauls, and Carthaginians knew the Etruscans for their fine metal craft. Metalworking in Etruria dates back to the Bronze Age, thanks to the high-quality ores of Tuscany, especially the copper and tin deposits of the Colline Metallifere, La Tolfa, and Monte Amiata.

The factories of Vulci, an important bronze-working center, specialized in and exported vessels of sheetmetal. Bossed-rim basins went out to southern Italy, Sicily, and Europe. Cups and jugs for wine service accompanied Tuscan wines to Gaul. Greek vessels and uten-

41. BRONZE BASIN HANDLE

Cortona, 5th century BC
L. 9.6 cm
MS 2314

This bronze handle was cast in a factory at Vulci and exported to Etruscan Cortona. Its sheet metal basin has not survived.

sils may have been more delicately decorated, but Etruscan goods offered sturdy (and valuable) solid bronze handles and bases. The Greeks admired Etruscan metalworkers greatly, calling them

42. GOLD ORNAMENT
7th century BC
H. 1 cm
MS 3350

This tiny gold bird, decorated with granulation, may have originally belonged to a rare, large brooch of Orientalizing style.

philotechnoi, skilled craftsmen who loved their work.

The Etruscans learned the craft of goldsmithing from the Phoenicians and Syrians. By the 6th century BC they were producing lavish quantities of gold jewelry of intricate and innovative design. Although they did not invent it, Etruscans became masters of the decorative technique called granulation.

Stoneworking

Stone sculpture began in Etruria only after contact with Phoenicians and Greeks. Thus, many features of Etruscan statues imitate foreign styles. The stones of Etruria were coarser than those of the East, however, and the local volcanic rocks, with large voids and inclusions, affected the style of carving. Broader outlines, softer hair or manes, and fewer surface details are typical. Sometimes a plaster coating was applied to the coarse stone, with clothing and ornaments painted on the smoother surface.

43. NENFRO LION
6th century BC
H. 62.5 cm
59-24-1

A tomb guardian figure, this fragmentary winged lion is of the volcanic stone and style common to Vulci's territory. It illustrates the early assimilation of the difficult techniques of stone sculpture learned from Syrians and Greeks in the 7th century BC and perfected during the 6th century BC.

Trade

The Etruscans' reputation as sea-farers and commercial competitors of the Greeks and Romans was widespread. By the 7th century BC painted vases from Greece depict battles between Etruscan merchants and pirates in Greek-style warships. Etruscan shipwrecks found off the coasts of Italy, Sardinia, and France produce a suprising assortment of Greek vases alongside Etruscan amphoras filled with produce. Etruscan products of pottery and bronze appear in sites throughout the Mediterranean. The Greek philosopher Aristotle tells us that the Etruscans and Carthaginians signed treaties pledging alliance for purposes of trade.

So many Greek vases have been excavated from Etruscan tombs that archaeologists once assumed they had been made in Etruria. Now that sources of pottery clays can be identified and styles are better understood, we know that Greek potters exported their wares in quantity to an avid mar-

44. BUCCHERO KANTHAROS
Vulci, Tomb B, 6th century BC
H. with handle, 12 cm
MS 1284

The one-handled cup (*kyathos*) and the two-handled cup (*kantharos*) are two of Etruria's most common vase shapes. Exported examples are found in Mediterranean shipwrecks of the 7th–6th century BC as well as in many Greek cities and sanctuaries. Both shapes were imitated by Athenian potters.

ket of collectors and social climbers in Etruria. As they became familiar with Etruscan tastes, Greek potters altered some of their products to please the Etruscan consumer. They imitated Etruscan shapes, painted them with popular Etruscan themes, and shipped them off to Italy.

The transfer of goods or ideas was not always commercial, however. Villanovan armor and Archaic Etruscan metal vessels, for example, have been found at Greek shrines like Olympia and Samos. These might be trophies taken by colonial Greeks in forgotten wars, but they could also be the offerings of Etruscan voyagers at foreign shrines. Many of the *fibulae* found in votive deposits in the Aegean may be all that remains from offerings of clothing made by Italian visitors to those shores.

We may never know how many people moved back and forth, intermarrying and raising children in two cultures, but we can be sure that some of the cultural riches of Etruria came from foreign associations.

45. BRONZE "NEGAU" HELMET

5th century BC
H. 18 cm
MS 1609

Arms and armor were exported from Vulci and Arezzo to Europe. Etruscan-made "Negau" (named for the find site in modern Slovenia) helmets were inspired by the armor of marauding Gauls. The helmets were eventually shipped north from Etruria by early "arms dealers" to the barbaric tribes of Gaul, Germany, and Scandinavia. This helmet has fine horse and lion projections which probably helped anchor straps.

RELIGION

Etruscans believed theirs to be a revealed religion, communicated to them by the gods of the sky, earth, and the underworld. These forces spoke to mortals through nature and its events: the flight of birds, the sound of thunder, the strikes of lightning bolts, and the entrails of sacrificed animals.

The many modes of learning the gods' messages brought forth different kinds of prophets. *Augurs*, for example, read the flight of birds. *Haruspices* scrutinized the livers of sacrificed sheep for signs of divine disapproval. Etruscans were famous for the way they carried out this rite: unlike their contemporaries, they removed the liver from the slaughtered animal before they examined it. After the divination, the animal's remains were divided among gods, priests, and people, and consumed.

At Etruscan sanctuaries, grateful worshippers heaped offerings on altars or in special pits. An offering might be a piece of jewelry or other prized possession, but it might also be a special kind of object made for votive use. Bronze or terracotta figurines or models were common: images of gods or goddesses, of suppliants, perhaps of a wished-for baby. Most common of all were terracotta models of the body parts for which healing was sought.

The Etruscans knew many kinds of gods, from spirits of nature and the underworld and invisible sky gods to deities who took on human form. Some of the Etruscan gods who were seen and depicted in human form were shared with Romans and Greeks (see box below).

The Etruscan Pantheon

ETRUSCAN	ROMAN	GREEK
Tin	Jupiter	Zeus
Uni	Juno	Hera
Menrva	Minerva	Athena
Sethlans	Vulcanus	Hephaistos
Turan	Venus	Aphrodite
Maris(?)	Mars	Ares
Turms	Mercurius	Hermes
Nethuns	Neptunus	Poseidon
Fufluns	Bacchus	Dionysos
Cel	Tellus(?)	Ge, Gaia
Selvans	Silvanus	
Usil	Sol	Helios
Tiur	Luna	Selene
Aplu	Apollo	Apollo
Aritimi, Artumes	Diana	Artemis

46. ETRUSCAN RED-FIGURED CUP

Falerii (Città Castellana), 4th century BC
Diam. 28 cm
MS 3444

The god Fufluns (Dionysos) appears with a maenad, one of his followers, on this cup made in Falerii.

47. BRONZE VOTIVE FIGURINE

Said to be from Tuscania, 6th century BC
H. 9.4 cm
MS 3496

This partially draped youth is a finely made figurine. A heavy loop below his plinth would have been set into a base for display.

48. VOTIVES

TERRACOTTA VOTIVE HEAD
3rd–2nd centuries BC
H. 21 cm
MS 5756

TERRACOTTA VOTIVE HEAD
3rd century BC
H. 21.7 cm
MS 5757

TERRACOTTA VOTIVE HEAD
2nd century BC
H. 14.8 cm
MS 5752

BRONZE VOTIVE FACIAL PLAQUE
3rd–2nd centuries BC
W. 7.3 cm
MS 1630

TERRACOTTA VOTIVE FOOT
3rd–2nd centuries BC
L. 22.4 cm
L-64-551

TERRACOTTA VOTIVE FOOT
3rd–2nd centuries BC
L. 22 cm
L-64-478

TERRACOTTA VOTIVE FOOT
3rd–2nd centuries BC
L. 24.1 cm
L-64-553

The male head is shown covered, as in Roman worship. The female half-head is a common design, probably made to hang on a wall. The head from a swaddled infant was probably offered in gratitude for the birth of a child. The bronze plaque sought healing for the nose and eyes. After heads, the most frequently offered "anatomical votives" are hands and feet. These were often injured by farmers, warriors, and ordinary people who worked hard. Two of the feet, and perhaps the third as well, show bunions.

49. TERRACOTTA VOTIVE HEAD
Early 5th century BC
H. 22 cm
MS 1830

This female head is one of the earliest
votive models, made from molds used to
create temple antefixes.

50. TERRACOTTA ACROTERION
6th–5th century BC
H. 22 cm
MS 1832

Acroteria, guardian statues of gods
and monsters, stalked the crests of
roofs.

SACRED ARCHITECTURE

Etruscan architecture looked quite
different from the familiar stone temples and gleaming marble statuary of
Greek architecture. Constrained by a
lack of fine stone, Etruscans built their
temples of wood, with terracotta roofs
and ornaments. Today the wooden su-
perstructures have almost entirely dis-
integrated. Only the stone foundations
and the terracotta roofs and decorations remain. Fortunately, the size and
types of terracottas can often tell us
what the whole building looked like,
and something of its history.

Roman writers described an Etruscan temple as a high podium on which
rose a broad, square building with
gabled roof, wide overhang, and deep
porch. Inside, three dark chambers
ended in solid walls. In front of the
temple was an augural area, where
priests stood to observe messages
from the gods in the flight of birds.

A tiled roof protected the perish-
able wooden or mudbrick building
blocks below. Half-round "cover"
tiles protected the joints of a first
layer of flat "pan" tiles. The end of a
row of cover tiles was capped with a
terracotta antefix. An array of terracotta fittings shielded important
beams and joints. Revetments included frieze plaques to cover longitudi-
nal beams, and gutters or simas to
draw off rainwater. Beam ends,
where exposed to the elements, were
sheathed with rectangular *columen* or
mutulus plaques.

51. TERRACOTTA ANTEFIX WITH SATYR HEAD
Caere (Cerveteri), 4th century BC
W. 46 cm
MS 1804

This antefix and the one on the facing page, with backdrops in the shape of shells, came from a large temple in the countryside of Caere (Cerveteri).

52. TERRACOTTA ANTEFIX WITH FEMALE HEAD
Caere (Cerveteri), 4th century BC
W. 50.2 cm
MS 1803

Female heads alternated with those of satyrs along the edge of the roof. The satyrs have red flesh that shows that they are males, while the female heads were painted with either white or black skin and wore large earrings that were fashionable in the 5th–4th centuries BC.

53. TERRACOTTA REVETMENT PLAQUE

Caere (Cerveteri), 4th century BC
H. 62.8 cm
MS 1806

This large *cortina pendula* (hanging curtain) was made to cover a horizontal beam. Its painted surface emphasizes the repeated floral pattern. Several holes, for use in attaching the plaque to the beam, are preserved.

54. ETRUSCAN RED-FIGURED JUG
4th century BC
H. 35.5 cm
MS 2517

This jug depicts a religious scene with Lasa, an altar, and a woman with a *tympanon* (drum).

55. AMPHORA
Orvieto, 3rd century BC
MS 2511
H. 36 cm

This amphora with handles in the shape of hippo-camps (half-horse, half-fish monsters) originally looked rather gaudy. It is a painted version of a type produced in "silvered ceramic." With its bright, fragile colors, it could not have been used in everyday life.

FINAL DAYS

Life in Etruria from the 4th through 1st centuries BC was still marked by affluent cities and productive countryside, but vast changes occurred in political and social life. Slave revolts and a growing class of wealthy freedmen and freedwomen accompanied the loss of the cities' autonomy to Rome. The tombs of aristocrats, commoners, and freedmen and freedwomen show a high level of technology and an ever increasing rate of literacy, but the days of the warrior-ruler and the princess who wove her family's clothing were over.

Eventually a new order would emerge with Etruscans holding posts under the Roman government. For status and fulfillment many turned to religious administration.

By the 1st century BC Etruria was just another part of the Roman world. Her warriors had become priests and authors, her weaver women owners of factories and patrons of the arts. Their families' futures lay with the power of Rome. Etruscan culture had flourished for the span of a millennium; its vestiges remain in the cities of Renaissance Tuscany, in Italy's tiled roofs and political and religious symbols, and in our own thought and writing.

56. ALABASTER CINERARY URN

3rd–2nd centuries BC
L. 62 cm
MS 2458A, B

This urn depicts Arnth Remzna, who perhaps was the administrator of a college of priests. The heads on sarcophagi and urns such as this were only generalized images, so while Remzna is depicted with a double chin, we cannot be sure he looked this way in life. The "obese Etruscan" was a character type. As in the art of some other cultures, the image of an obese person was recognized as a symbol of wealth.

57. GLASS BOWL

Tuscania tomb, 3rd–2nd centuries BC
Diam. 13.2 cm
MS 1506

This fine ribbed bowl formed the centerpiece of a Tuscania lady's belongings. Glass, made in Etruria as early as the late 8th–7th centuries BC, now began to come into its own for containers of all sorts.

58. SARCOPHAGUS WITH RECLINING MALE

Città Musarna, 3rd–2nd centuries BC
L. 203 cm
MS 3488

This coffin lid shows a man reclining as if at a banquet, still the favorite symbol for an important, socially connected personage in Etruria's final days. The sea monsters that decorate the chest illustrate the growing trend in late Etruscan art toward simple, repeated images and away from complicated narrative with human figures. (The lid and chest probably do not belong together.)

59. NENFRO BUST OF FEMALE

Tuscania tomb, 3rd–2nd centuries BC
H. 44 cm
MS 1428

The personal belongings found in the tomb indicate burials of women. This imposing bust might represent one of the deceased. More likely, it is meant to be a goddess of the afterlife, perhaps "Vei thval" ("Vei who will reveal"). Nenfro is a local volcanic stone.

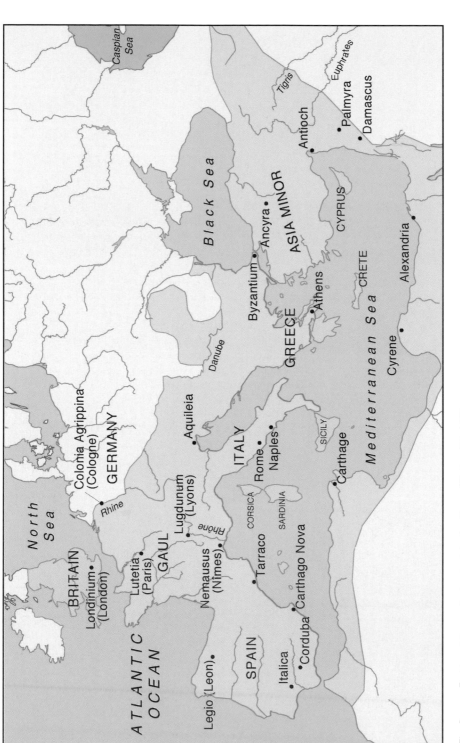

The Roman Empire at its greatest extent, in the time of Trajan (AD 117).

3

The Roman World

Roman civilization traced its roots back to nearly 1000 BC and lasted in one form or another until 500 AD. During this time it spread from the tiny settlement that became the city of Rome to master a world that reached to the edge of Central Asia and included much of Europe. Rome's republican government (509–31 BC) had a profound effect on the formation of our own constitution. Its imperial government, initiated by the emperor Augustus (27 BC–AD 14), established a model for all subsequent world empires. No less importantly, Latin literature and Roman art have provided the foundation for much of the development of Western arts and letters since the Renaissance.

The demise of the western Roman Empire was a gradual process brought on by the resulting disorder of a politically weakened empire split between east and west, various incursions of barbaric tribes who reached the city of Rome itself in AD 410, and a general economic crisis.

60. The Roman Forum looking southeast. The Forum was the heart of religious, commercial, and civic life in Rome from Republican through late Imperial times.

Courtesy of I. B. Romano.

61. SILVER *TETRADRACHM* OF
AUGUSTUS (27 BC–AD 14)
Ca. 24–20 BC
Diam. 2.8 cm
29-126-888

THE ROMAN EMPERORS

The Roman Republic had a representative form of government that divided power between the Senate and two consuls presiding over an array of lesser magistrates. It lasted from its traditional beginning in 509 BC until 31 BC when it was reorganized by Octavius (later called Augustus) after many years of brutal civil war.

Augustus installed a form of government which kept the Senate and consuls, but placed power effectively in the hands of a supreme ruler, the emperor, who was to hold that power for life. He himself ruled for 45 years. Fifty-one emperors followed Augustus, some ruling for more than two decades, others for only days. The Roman Empire itself lasted for over three and a half centuries. Imperial rule may be divided into five dynasties, separated by periods of disruption or anarchy.

The Julio-Claudians

The reign of the Julio-Claudian emperors (31 BC–AD 68) began with the restoration of order under Octavius.

62. GOLD *AUREUS* OF VESPASIAN
(AD 69–79)
AD 69–70
Diam. 1.8 cm
29-126-937

Heir of his great-uncle Julius Caesar, Octavius spent 13 years eliminating his rivals and taking sole control of the Roman state. In 27 BC he took the title of Augustus (revered). This completed the dismantlement of the Republic and Augustus's transition to emperor. After his death the Senate awarded him divine honors. Augustus's successors are among the most famous or notorious of the Roman emperors—Tiberius, Caligula, Claudius, and Nero.

63. GOLD *AUREUS* OF HADRIAN
(AD 117–138)
AD 125–128
Diam. 1.9 cm
29-126-965

64. GOLD *AUREUS* OF SEPTIMIUS
SEVERUS (AD 193–211)
AD 193
Diam. 1.9 cm
29-126-1049

The Flavians (AD 69–96)

Vespasian was the first of the Flavian emperors. Raised to power by the legions in the east, he was successful in his campaigns on the northern frontier, naturally industrious, and pointedly simple in his personal habits. These qualities led the Senate to proclaim him a god after his death. He was succeeded by his sons Titus and Domitian.

The "Adoptive Emperors"

The emperors (AD 96–180) who succeeded the Flavians were related not by blood, but through adoption. Among them are the so-called Five Good Emperors, including Trajan and Hadrian. Hadrian's notable successors, Antoninus Pius and Marcus Aurelius, are also counted among the "good" emperors. The dynasty came to a bad end with the reign of an incompetent youth, Marcus Aurelius's son Commodus.

Commodus and the Severans (AD 180–235)

The disastrous reign of the cruel Commodus ended in assassination. One of his successors, a North African military professional called Septimius Severus, was proclaimed emperor after the murder of Didius Julianus. He died of natural causes in York. The murder of the last Severan, Alexander Severus, ended the dynasty and ushered in the next period, a half century of near total anarchy.

Third-century Anarchy

During the political chaos of the third century (AD 235–284), emperors followed one another in rapid succession, Aurelian among them. Aurelian was of peasant stock from Illyria and he possessed the requisite energy and military skills for restoring the empire after decades of political turmoil. His career was cut short when he was murdered in a military plot.

Diocletian through Constantine

The anarchy of the 3rd century (AD 284-337) was finally brought under control by Diocletian and his ambitious military, economic, and legal policies. His rule set the stage for the empire's eventual split into its western and eastern parts under Constantine the Great. Constantine is renowned for the Edict of Milan, which in AD 313 recognized Christianity as a lawful religion. In 330 he chose Byzantium as his new imperial capital, renaming it Constantinople. He was baptized as he lay dying peacefully at the age of 67.

65. GOLD *SOLIDUS* OF CONSTANTINE I (AD 306–337)
AD 326–330
Diam. 2.0 cm
29-126-1178

66. MARBLE HEAD OF THE EMPEROR CONSTANTIUS II (?)
El Bab, northeast of Aleppo, Syria, ca. AD 337–361
H. 29 cm
L-51-1

The royal diadem in the hair and comparisons with his coins suggest that this is a portrait of Constantius II, the third son of Constantine the Great. Constantius was driven to put to death Gallus, his cousin and co-regent, on suspicion of treachery. He perished seven years later in Asia Minor while racing to confront the challenge of his rival, Julian the Apostate.

On loan from the Max von Oppenheim Foundation.

THE PUTEOLI MARBLE BLOCK

This marble block was originally used for an honorific inscription that was later chiseled off, making it nearly unreadable today. The inscription lauded the emperor Domitian for his civic and military achievements, alluding to something he did (probably new road construction) for the town of Puteoli. In fact, Domitian was a paranoid and cruel emperor who sought to take away too much power from the Roman Senate. He was assassinated in AD 96. His memory was condemned by the Senate and all public trace of his rule, including this inscription, was expunged in an official act of *damnatio memoriae*.

The erased inscription reads:

IMP CAESARI
"To the Imperator Caesar
DIVI VESPASIANI F
Son of the deified Vespasian,
DOMITIANO AVG
Domitian Augustus
GERMAN PONT MAX
victor in Germany, Pontifex Maximus,
TRIB POTEST XV IMP XXII
holding the power of Tribune for the fifteenth year,
Imperator for the twenty-second time,
COS XVII CENS PERPET P P
Consul for the seventeenth time, Perpetual Censor, Father of the country,
COLONIA FLAVIA AVG
the Flavian Augustan colony
PVTEOLANA
of Puteoli [dedicates this]
INDVLGENTIA MAXIMI
by the indulgence of the Great
DIVINIQVE PRINCIPIS
and Divine Princeps,
VRBI EIVS ADMOTA
(something) having been moved closer to his city"

Not long after the inscription on Side A was defaced, the back of the Puteoli block was carved into a relief panel and mounted on an arch to honor the celebrated Trajan. Depicted are three soldiers in parade dress who are members of the emperor Trajan's personal bodyguard, the Praetorian Guard. Trajan himself would have appeared above or below them, but only this portion of the arch survives (an adjacent fragment is in the Berlin Museum). The defaced inscription to the emperor Domitian and Trajan's Praetorian guard, back to back, remind us that an emperor's power depended directly upon the support of his army.

67. THE PUTEOLI MARBLE BLOCK
Side A: Erased inscription honoring Domitian
Puteoli (modern Pozzuoli), southern Italy, AD 95/96
H. 162 cm
MS 4916

68. THE PUTEOLI MARBLE BLOCK
Side B: Marble relief from a Trajanic arch
Puteoli (modern Pozzuoli), Italy, AD 102
H. 162 cm
MS 4916

69. MARBLE HEAD OF A HELMETED ROMAN LEGIONARY

1st–2nd centuries AD
H. 35.5 cm
54-3-1

On the cap of the helmet is a small relief emblem of the foreparts of a winged horse, Pegasos. We know from Roman military records that three Roman legions used the Pegasos emblem: Legio I Adiutrix, Legio II Adiutrix, and Legio III Augusta. This sculpture was probably a part of a commemorative monument relating to one of these legions.

70. MARBLE MASK OF A
WATER DEITY

Teanum Sidicinum, northern
Campania, Italy, second half of
1st–2nd centuries AD
H. 75 cm
MS 4917

This mask of a bearded, hoary
old man may personify either
Oceanus or a river, like Father
Tiber. It was found in a
Roman public bath, where it
was used for a fountain
waterspout.

ROMAN RELIGION

Roman religion was a complex weave of cultic threads. The earliest Romans believed in animism, the divine powers residing in nature and the human environment. As time went on they expanded their religious horizons through contact with their Etruscan and South Italian and Sicilian Greek neighbors, whose gods took human forms and personalities. When adopted by the Romans these anthropomorphic Greco-Etruscan deities, with new names like Jupiter, Juno, and Mars, became the Roman pantheon familiar to us today.

By the late 3rd century BC a stream of strange and exotic Oriental and Egyptianizing cults such as that of Cybele, the Anatolian mother goddess, and of the Egyptian Isis and Serapis began to appear in Rome as her political domination of the Mediterranean basin spread. The Romans steadily added new deities to honor a wide range of abstract social forces such as Dea Roma, the personification of the spirit of Rome; Concordia, the goddess of "Harmonius Agreement"; and Victoria, the Roman equivalent of the Greek Nike.

With the advent of the Imperial state in 31 BC the Romans embarked on three centuries of worship of their supreme rulers. The first emperor, Augustus, refused official deification, but, as the adopted son of the already deified Caesar, his divinization was

72. BRONZE FIGURINE OF MERCURY

1st–2nd centuries AD
H. 10.8 cm
48-2-223

71. BRONZE PRIAPIC HERM

Iconion, Turkey, 1st century AD
H. 23.4 cm
48-2-271

Priapus is the rural god of vegetation and fertility, linked with the worship of Venus. Wearing a low cap, the woodland god's beardless head is encircled by a vine that descends down either side to cross over his erect phallus. The piece may have been a furniture attachment or a decorative part of a chariot.

Mercury was a Campano-Etruscan god of commerce and transportation. His cult was established in Rome in 495 BC. Under the empire his likeness was often blended with that of the emperor in statues.

inevitable upon his death. A select group of subsequent emperors and their family members were also given the honor of deification.

The monotheistic religions of Judaism and Christianity grew in popularity as the Roman Empire expanded, and relations between the Roman state and the Jews or Christians altered with historic and political events. The monotheistic beliefs and seemingly strange religious practices of the Jews, such as keeping the Sabbath holy, circumcision, and dietary restrictions, inevitably collided with official Roman practices. Also, the refusal of Jews and Christians to accept the notion of the emperor as god created a climate of suspicion. But although at first the Roman state looked upon early Christians as an underclass of potentially dangerous revolutionaries, eventually, under the emperor Constantine (AD 306–337), Christianity became the favored religion.

73. BRONZE HEAD OF SOL
2nd–3rd centuries AD
H. 8.2 cm
48-2-268

Although broken from its body, the hollow-cast head is nearly intact. Only the radiate crown, detectable as broken stumps behind the raised locks of hair, is missing. Sol, the sun god, was introduced to Rome as Sol Indiges (the Heroic Sun). The Syrian cult of Sol Invictus (the Invincible Sun), arrived after AD 68. Popular with later Roman emperors, his image was eventually merged with the triumphant risen Christ.

74. MARBLE HEAD OF A PRIEST OF THE IMPERIAL CULT
Possibly from Caesarea (Kayseri), Turkey, late 3rd century AD
H. 31.5 cm
MS 215

Tiny busts of 11 divinities decorate the figured crown. This type of crown seems to be most at home in Asia Minor, where it is frequently but not exclusively associated with the Imperial cult.

Worship of the Gods

Like their Etruscan and Greek neighbors, the Romans built temples to house the images of their more important deities and established elaborate sanctuaries in places believed to have been touched by particular gods and goddesses. Like their neighbors, they maintained regular contact with the gods through acts of sacrifice and implored their benevolent intervention through gifts called votives.

Votives are gifts given to the gods to ensure a favorable response to prayers or as thanks for favors already granted. They appear in all sizes, from tiny figurines to greater than life-size statues. Some are images of the gods or portrayals of subjects associated with the gods, such as the eagle with Jupiter or the lion with Cybele, the Great Mother. Others represent priests or priestesses or, as is often the case, ordinary worshippers. They also represent the kinds of edible animal and vegetable products believed to be especially pleasing to the gods.

75. MARBLE GOD OR DIVINIZED EMPEROR
Probably from Rome, 1st–early 2nd centuries AD
H. 160 cm
MS 4018

This figure was adapted from a familiar Greek Hermes type of the later 4th century BC. The body may have been joined with the portrait head of a divinized emperor. The missing head was turned toward the upraised right hand which perhaps held a spear.

76. CARNELIAN STAMP SEAL

2nd century BC
W. 2.1 cm
29-128-900

A bearded soldier, armed with helmet, body armor, shield, and lance, holds a *patera* (sacrificial dish) over a garlanded round altar. The heads of two more soldiers and a sacrificial ox appear in the background. The gold setting is modern.

77. UMBRO-ETRUSCAN TERRACOTTA VOTIVE SET

Todi, north of Rome, 3rd century BC
Diam. 31.5 cm
MS 1407–1423, MS 1425–1427

An offering tray filled with symbolic miniaturized foodstuffs and cooking wares. Tuder (modern Todi) was an Etruscan city under Roman rule on the border of Umbria and Tuscany.

78. BRONZE VOTIVE BULL

1st–3rd centuries AD
H. 5.1 cm
48-2-103

In herding cultures like those of the Anatolian plateau, bulls are an age-old sign of strength, fertility, and wealth. They are also associated with specific cults such as that of Jupiter Dolichenus and Cybele.

79. View of Lake Nemi. Roman nobility, including Julius Caesar and emperor Caligula (AD 37–41), had lavish villas along the shores of the lake. Caligula kept two enormous floating pleasure barges near his villa.

Courtesy of I. B. Romano.

The Sanctuary of Diana Nemorensis

The Sanctuary of Diana Nemorensis lies on the northern side of Lake Nemi, a volcanic lake surrounded by the wooded slopes of the Alban Hills, 20 kilometers. southeast of Rome. Worship at Nemi began as early as the 5th century BC. The height of Diana's cult dates from the late 3rd century BC to the 2nd century AD. The succession of the priesthood of Diana's

80. MARBLE CULT STATUE HEAD, PROBABLY OF DIANA
Late 2nd century BC
H. 44.7 cm
MS 3483

The idealized, conservative style and the large scale suggest this head was part of a cult statue from one of Nemi's major temples. It was originally adorned with a diadem of another material, probably bronze.

81. LOWER TORSO OF A MARBLE STATUETTE OF DIANA

Late 2nd–1st centuries BC
H. with plinth 55 cm
MS 3453

Many small votive statuettes of Diana in marble and bronze survived at the site. Most show her in the company of a hunting dog or deer and wearing the archetypal costume of the huntress: a short *chiton* with a *himation* tied around her waist, short leather boots, a quiver for her arrows, and a bow or spear or torch.

82. MARBLE GRIFFIN CAULDRON

Sanctuary of Diana at Lake Nemi,
1st century AD
H. 62 cm
MS 3448

Eight solid marble vessels were excavated from the Sanctuary of Diana Nemorensis. All were inscribed CHIO D D, or *Chio Donum Dedit* (Chio gave the gift). Four are in the shape of cauldrons, Greek wine-mixing bowls, with griffin heads. All eight vessels would have been dedicated at the same time.

cult at Nemi was linked to the possession of a mythic golden bough from an oak tree in her sacred grove.

Diana was worshipped at Nemi in her guise as the goddess of the hunt, but her cult was complex. She was associated with Hekate, the goddess of the underworld, and with the Egyptian goddess Isis.

She was also a healing divinity. Suppliants seeking cures or protection from illness deposited terracotta votives shaped like various body parts at the sanctuary. According to myth, Asklepios, the Greek god of medicine, restored the hero Hippolytos to life in the guise of Virbius, the servant of Diana.

The sanctuary seems to have attracted women worshippers in particular. The nature of the votive gifts to Diana reflects their attendance: jewelry and women's clothing, including silk and sequined tunics and gold belts.

83. MARBLE STATUETTE OF A DANCING FAUN (?)
Sanctuary of Diana at Lake Nemi, late 2nd–1st centuries BC
H. 66 cm
MS 3465

Marble statuettes of the woodland creatures of Diana's world form a large part of the Museum's Nemi collection. They include depictions of fauns or satyrs and young, effeminate, nude male figures whose identity is disputed.

84. PLAQUE WITH MASKS OF A SATYR AND DIONYSOS
1st century AD
L. 44 cm
MS 3459

This is one of four marble plaques from Nemi with theater-like masks. The mask on the right represents a youthful, effeminate Dionysos.

85. View of the excavations of Minturnae, looking east showing the Etrusco-Italic temple remains in the foreground. The Via Appia is in the background, marked by a row of pines.

Courtesy of Valentina Livi.

COLONIA MINTURNAE

Minturnae lies 65 kilometers northwest of Naples, where the Via Appia crosses the Garigliano (ancient Liris) River on the border between Latium and Campania. Originally inhabited by Italic tribesmen called the Aurunci, it was conquered by the Romans in 313 BC. Eighteen years later it was colonized as a *colonia civium Romanorum*, intended to serve as a small military outpost.

In the Republican period such outposts were typically made up of 4,500 to 6,000 men drawn from both the urban population of Rome and the neighboring Latin cities. In addition to securing points of strategic military interest, they also helped to provide land for the Italian peasantry. Their occupants retained Roman citizenship.

Minturnae soon grew to a respectable size, only to be badly damaged by fires. It was recolonized by Augustus with demobilized veterans. Thereafter it enjoyed a long existence until its final abandonment about AD 590.

Architectural terracotta decorations make up the Museum's most exceptional category of finds from Minturnae. Although typical of central and northern Italo-Etruscan buildings, such decorations are rarely found in museums outside of Italy.

The once colorfully painted revetments are part of a native Italic crafts tradition. Largely uninfluenced by Greek stoneworking methods, artisans in central Italy continued to work with terracotta until the end of the Republic in 31 BC and even beyond. Conservative traditionalists like Cato the Elder (243–149 BC) praised the technique. He berated his countrymen for preferring flashier Greek bronzes and marbles to the "old terracotta images of the gods" and, by implication, decorations like these. Nevertheless, architectural terracottas eventually lost their appeal and disappeared. Minturnae marks the furthest south that they have been found.

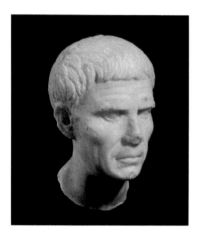

86. PORTRAIT OF A MIDDLE-AGED MAN

Minturnae, SW corner, Temple B,
third quarter of 1st century BC
H. 21 cm
32-36-64

Some have identified this head as
Julius Caesar, but it more likely
represents a citizen of local impor-
tance. Its small size suggests it
belonged to a bust rather than a
complete statue and was intended
to commemorate someone who
had died.

87. PORTRAIT OF DRUSUS OR GERMANICUS

Minturnae, SW corner, Temple B,
late 1st century BC–ca. AD 20
H. 41.5 cm
32-36-66

A portrait of either Drusus, Augustus's
favorite general and stepson, or German-
icus, Drusus's own eldest son. Both
would have been popular with Minturnae's colony of war veterans. Both
were considered possible successors to
Augustus's throne. Either might have
received posthumous honors in nearby
Temple A, which seems to have housed a
cult honoring Rome and the royal family.

88. PAINTED CORNICE

Minturnae, Temple of
Jupiter, 3rd century BC
L. 74 cm
32-36-3

Part of the temple's terracotta roof decoration. A
row of these elements
would have had perforated
plaques above and hanging
plaques below, all colorfully
painted black, white, and
red.

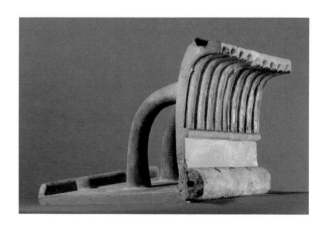

89. The civic forum and principal temple of the Roman city of Dougga, beautifully situated on the hillslopes of north-central Tunisia. Dougga lies in the heart of what was the Roman province of Africa Proconsularis, and served as a granary for Rome during the Imperial period.

Courtesy of D. White.

TRADE AND INDUSTRY UNDER THE EMPIRE

The Romans brought travel and communications to an unprecedented level during the 1st and 2nd centuries AD. They cleared the seas of pirates and developed a network of all-weather roads. Trade flourished.

Well-planned colonial cities sprang up in North Africa and across Europe and Britain. Their religious and civic centers, broad streets, adequate housing, and good sanitation rivaled those in the cities of Italy. Many of the old eastern Mediterranean centers enjoyed substantial state-subsidized improvements.

The Roman state administered the best farming and stock-raising areas, forest lands, mines, and quarries. Fish-ing grounds produced surpluses of freshwater and saltwater fish unimaginable today. Parts of North Africa supported agriculture where today there is only desert, while France and Spain routinely exported wheat, wine, and olive surpluses.

The impact of slavery on the economy of the Roman world was vast. It is estimated that one person out of every three was a slave. Public slaves built roads, cleaned sewers, and repaired aqueducts. Private slaves worked in domestic houses or on farms. Most actors, musicians, circus performers, and gladiators were slaves. Many typically "Roman" products, such as glass and pottery, were manufactured primarily by slaves, who were most likely Greeks, Gauls, or Africans by birth.

Roman Coinage

In a pre-newspaper age coins provided a convenient means for the state to disseminate its authorized messages to the Roman people. Their condensed imagery and simplified abbreviations conveyed complex information to audiences not necessarily conversant with Latin. Their portraits have left us with a gallery of some of antiquity's greatest heroes as well as its blackest villains. Control of the mint placed finances squarely in the hands of the state.

Republican Period Coins

The Romans started producing their own coins only around 300 BC, well after coinage had been introduced elsewhere in the Mediterranean area. These heavy bronze coins were gradually reduced in size as wars at home and abroad put increasing demands on the use of bronze for arms and armor. Silver and, more rarely, gold coins were also struck. As part of the reform of 211 BC, a new silver denomination, the *denarius* (equal to 10 *asses*, began to be issued in great quantity. It became the Roman coin par excellence for the next five centuries.

90. BRONZE *AS*
Ca. 225 BC
Diam. 6.3 cm
29-126-873A

Ship's prow. The *as* is a coin denomination that originally weighed one Roman pound.

Roman Imperial Coins to AD 275

Under the empire, bronze and copper coins were used for everyday marketplace transactions. They were issued in several denominations, distinguished by size and metal color. Under Nero (ca. AD 64), denominations were further distinguished by the type of crown worn by the emperor. Along with silver coins, gold coins now circulated widely, in part because of their 99% purity. They were struck under strict imperial control.

The Roman emperors modified the system of coinage several times. In AD 215, for example, the *denarius* was replaced by a "double *denarius*" consisting of 75% silver and 25% copper. By AD 275 silver coins were virtually nonexistent. *Denarii* were minted in billon (copper alloyed with just enough silver to give it a silvery-yellow appearance).

Roman Imperial Coins after AD 275

A serious overhaul of Roman coinage began in AD 275. The emperors Aurelian (AD 270–275) and Diocletian (AD 284–305) both attempted currency reforms to combat rising prices and devastating inflation. Gold was put into wide circulation once again, at over 97% purity. Although the amount of silver they contained increased slightly, billon issues were not widely accepted and soon fell out of production. Bronze coins now had their denomination and the location of their mints identified by abbreviations. By the 4th century AD most silver and locally issued bronze coins were replaced by state-issued gold and bronze coins. The images on the reverses of the coins became more stereotyped, and the lettering and execution increasingly stylized.

obverse

reverse

91. REPUBLICAN PERIOD COINS (left to right):

SILVER *DIDRACHM*
225–214 BC
Diam. 2.2 cm
29-126-601
Obv.: Janiform head laureate.
Rev.: Jupiter and Victory in a four-horse chariot.
Inscr ROMA.

The *didrachm* is a Greek coin denomination adopted by the Romans.

SILVER *DENARIUS*
Publius Paetus, 138 BC
Diam. 2 cm
29-126-626
Obv.: Head of Roma.
Rev.: The Dioscuri (Castor and Pollux) on horseback.
Inscr. P. PAETVS ROMA.

Around 210 BC the Romans developed a new denomination, the *denarius*, which remained in use until about AD 275.

SILVER *DENARIUS*
Q. Pomponius Musa, 66 BC
Diam. 1.8 cm
29-126-781
Obv.: Head of Apollo.
Rev.: Clio, muse of History.
Inscr. to right Q. POMPONI, to left MVSA.

By the 2nd century BC minters began to personalize coin designs in anticipation of running for higher political office. This minter juxtaposed his name, Musa, with the image of a muse.

SILVER *DENARIUS*
Julius Caesar, 47–46 BC
Diam. 1.8 cm
29-126-823A
Obv.: Head of Venus.
Rev.: Aeneas holds the *palladium* (statue of Athena) while carrying his father, Anchises.
Inscr. CAESAR.

Caesar minted this coin in Africa, where he needed coins to pay his troops.

92. ROMAN IMPERIAL COINS TO AD 275

TOP LEFT: SILVER *DENARIUS*
Otho, AD 69
Diam. 2.0 cm
29-126-935
Personification of Security.
Inscr. SECVRITAS P R

Despite his attempt to reassure his followers with this image, Otho clung to power for only four months.

TOP RIGHT: COPPER *AS*
Domitian, AD 87
Diam. 2.8 cm
29-126-949
Domitian wearing a laurel crown.
Inscr. IMP CAES DOMIT AVG GERM COS XIII CENS PER P P or "successful General, Augustus, Conqueror of Germany, Consul for the 13th time, Censor Forever, Father of his Country."

BOTTOM LEFT: BRASS *SESTERTIUS*
Trajan, AD 103–111
Diam. 3.4 cm
29-126-960
Trajan wearing a laurel crown.
Inscr. IMP CAES NERVAE TRAIANO AVG GER DAC P M TR P COS V P P

The inscribed titles define the emperor's religious and political power base as well as his conquests in Germany and the Balkans.

BOTTOM RIGHT: BILLON DOUBLE *DENARIUS*
Aemilianus, AD 253
Diam. 2.2 cm
29-126-1087
Aemilianus wearing a radiate crown.
Inscr. IMP AEMILIANVS AVG.PIVS FEL.

Aemilianus is here prematurely proclaimed FELIX, "Fortunate." He held power for only a year.

93. ROMAN IMPERIAL COINS AFTER AD 275

TOP: BILLON DOUBLE *DENARIUS*
Aurelian, AD 270–275
Diam. 2.1 cm
29-126-1103
Holding a thunderbolt and bow, the sun god Sol tramples
on a captive.
Inscr. ORIENS AVG B XXIR*.

"XXIR" identifies this coin as a denarius minted at Rome.
The silver from the alloy has been lost.

BOTTOM RIGHT: BRONZE *FOLLIS*
Diocletian, AD 293
Diam. 2.6 cm
29-126-1138
Diocletian wearing a laurel crown.
Inscr. IMP C C VAL DIOCLETIANVS P F AVG

The remaining silver "wash" can be seen between the letters of the inscription.

BOTTOM LEFT: COPPER OR BRONZE *FOLLIS*
Maximianus as Caesar, AD 305–307
Diam. 2.6 cm
E 12952
Head of Maximianus.
Inscr. IMP C MAXIMIANVS P F AVG.

94. WINE TRANSPORT AMPHORA

Grand Congloué, second shipwreck,
ca. 110–80 BC
H. 104 cm
89-2-3

This amphora bears the stamp SES followed by an anchor. The renowned underwater explorer Jacques Cousteau recovered some 1,200 similarly stamped amphoras from the site off the southern coast of France. He concluded that most of the ship's wine cargo had been stored in amphoras produced by the wealthy Sestius family from Cosa, a port of Rome. Massive numbers of amphora handles stamped SES have been excavated there.

Maritime Trade

To judge from the number of shipwrecks recovered from Mediterranean waters, Roman maritime commerce reached its peak between 100 BC and AD 100. Barges and river-boats plied the Rhône, the Po, and the Tiber. A brisk trade on the Nile connected sub-Saharan Africa with the Mediterranean coast. The largest seagoing merchantmen of this period carried up to 500 tons and more, although most ancient shipping must have been far smaller.

The bulk goods normally transported by water ranged from regional agricultural commodities like grains, oils, and wines (shipped in barrels by the 3rd century AD) to consignments of lumber, marble, rooftiles, and other building materials. The trade in finished marble sarcophagi and statuary reached its all-time high during the first three centuries AD. Entirely prefabricated churches were shipped from the Asia Minor coast to destinations as far away as Sicily.

95. WINE TRANSPORT AMPHORA

Grand Congloué, second shipwreck,
ca. 110–80 BC
H. 104 cm
89-2-4

This amphora, like the one above, was found in a Mediterranean shipwreck by Jacques Cousteau. It is covered with traces of incrustation.

96. RED-GLOSS POTTERY

TOP: SOUTH GAULISH BOWL

Made in La Graufesenque, France, first half of 1st century AD
W. 10.1 cm
MS 4877A

Signed by M. Perenni Tigranus's slave, Saturninus. M. Perenni was himself a freed slave. On the right a man carries a sack over his left shoulder. The figure on the left has been interpreted as Socrates drinking the poison hemlock.

Roman Red-Gloss Pottery

Roman red-gloss pottery reached its peak in the early years of the empire. Arretine ware, produced at Arretium (modern Arezzo), dominated the market from the 1st century BC until about AD 60. The pottery was plain or decorated with molded leaves and garlands of flowers surrounding scenes of mythological figures and everyday life.

The successor Gaulish wares were decorated with human figures and running animals set inside paneled registers. During the 1st century AD major Gaulish pottery centers opened at Lyons, Lezoux, and La Graufesenque. By AD 50 these centers were exporting wares to nearly every part of the empire and beyond. By the end of the 1st century AD, potters in England, Germany, Switzerland, and Spain were copying Gaulish Red-Gloss.

By the 2nd century AD pottery centers sprang up in Tunisia and Algeria to produce African Red Slip. Lacking the glossy shine of earlier wares, it was for the most part plain, with grooves, rouletting, and simple appliqués depicting animal, hunting, and mythological subjects. Eastern Sigillata

BOTTOM: SOUTH GAULISH BOWL

Made in La Graufesenque, France, ca. AD 65–75
Diam. 13.8 cm
MS 4096

The tiny rivet hole bored into the wall shows that this piece was valued enough to be repaired in antiquity.

LEFT: EASTERN SIGILLATA B DISH

Beth Shean, Israel, AD 50–75
Diam. 12 cm
29-102-544

The shape of this Palestinian dish and the use of barbotine decoration are similar to dishes from the Rhine Region. They demonstrate the interconnection between widely separated regional pottery industries during the early empire.

RIGHT: GAULISH LION MORTARIUM

Late 2nd–early 3rd centuries AD
L. 9.1 cm
29-100-5

The rim and pouring spout of a heavy bowl or mortar used for food preparation. A lion's head decorates the spout.

(stamped) industries were active in the eastern Mediterranean from about 150 BC onward. Their production climaxed in the 5th to 7th centuries AD.

97. MOLD-BLOWN GLASS VESSELS
Late 1st century AD
H. of tallest vessel, 23 cm
MS 4980, MS 4993, MS 5114, MS 4990, 86-35-82

The Glass Industry

The Romans all but ignored glass as a material until the 1st century BC when blown glass was invented. There was not even a Latin word for it until about 65 BC. Yet scarcely a century later glass vessels could be found in virtually every Roman house. The glassworking craft had been transformed into an industry, with perhaps as many as 100 million vessels being made every year—everything from delicate perfume bottles to heavy storage jars, and all kinds of tableware.

The first glassworkers in Italy were slaves, Syrian and Judaean craftsmen shipped over as spoils of war around 10 BC. They brought with them the crafts of mold-casting and free-blowing that were essential for the glassworking industry's success. Their descendants, as freedmen, most likely ran the workshops that sprang up close to every provincial city and military camp throughout the empire. By the early 1st century AD, all the aesthetic techniques of our modern glass industry—among them mold-blowing, lathe-cutting, and faceting—were standard in the Roman glassworking repertoire.

Mold-blown glass made sturdy vessels suitable for short- and medium-range shipment of marketplace goods. Wine and olive oil, preserved fruits and cooking sauces, dried herbs and medicines were common contents. Compared with massive pottery amphoras, glass bottles figured little in long-range trade. Nevertheless, they often traveled far from where they were made. Filled and refilled, bottles were carted from town to town until they rested finally as storage vessels in some distant provincial kitchen. Glassware could travel

98. BRICKSTAMP
Late 3rd–early 4th centuries AD
L. 18 cm
MS 2152

Stamped FF AVGG ET CAESS NN on the outside, SR in the center.

long distances swiftly, however, if it was part of a military legion's transfer to a new trouble spot.

The invention of glassblowing around 70 BC and its industrial-scale use around the time of Christ made glassware affordable for all Romans. The wealthy stored their cosmetic and medicinal lotions in silver and bronze. Poorer folk could now use both pottery and glass.

Bottles called *unguentaria* were used to store oils or lotions. At first small and crudely finished, their shapes became greatly refined over the centuries. Various other kinds of glass juglets and jars stored herbal ingredients and oils so that lotions could be prepared fresh each morning.

The Brick Trade

For the next four centuries much of Rome, as well as the rest of Italy, relied heavily on bricks. Their manufacture became an important component of the economy. With bricks came brickstamps, rectangular at first, but eventually curved, circular, semicircular, and crescent shaped. They served as trademarks. When the names of the annual consuls were added between AD 110 and 164, they provided exceptionally accurate dates for the structures to which they were attached. By the early 3rd century AD they carried the names of the emperors, who by then owned most of the brickyards.

99. The peristyle of the House of the Vettii, Pompeii, Italy. AD 60–70.
Courtesy of D. White.

100. BRONZE DOOR
KNOCKER OR LIFTING RING
Beth Shean, Israel, late Roman
Imperial period
H. 13.5 cm
29-108-105

If this piece was used as a lifting
ring, it may have been on a chest.

DOMESTIC LIFE

It is impossible to generalize about
domestic life in the ancient Roman
world. The empire was vast. Climates,
natural resources, and customs varied
widely. The food, clothing, housing,
careers, and leisure activities in Roman
Britain or Gaul differed greatly from
those in the North African provinces or
the Roman East.

Life for the ordinary Roman was
not easy. The urban center of Rome
was the most sophisticated of ancient
cities. Nevertheless, the average citizen
of Rome lived in rented quarters in
multi-storeyed apartment complexes
called *insulae*. These were for the most
part crowded, squalid, noisy, and expensive. Except for a coal brazier, they
had no heat, no running water, and no
toilet facilities.

Most Romans, however, lived in
rural areas. Yet for the average farmer,
life was no better than for the urban

101. MOLD-PRESSED GLASS RELIEF PLAQUE
Possibly made in Rome, 1st–2nd centuries AD
H. 15 cm
MS 5656A

The image of the snaky-headed Medusa is a popular Greek and Roman apotropaic device to ward off evil and provide protection. Relief rondels of this type may have served as architectural ornament, inlaid into walls.

dweller. Farming was largely a family enterprise and women and children were expected to participate in the back-breaking work of farm chores. Mandatory military service took men away from farms for long periods of time. While the wealthy landowner could afford to purchase more slaves for laborers, the poor farmer was often forced to sell his land and look for employment in the already crowded cities.

The empire was rich, and many Romans prospered and filled their homes with the comforts of the well-to-do. For the most part, it is the remains of their life that fill museum collections. Remember, however, how few Romans shared in this kind of life.

The Roman House

Housing varied greatly throughout the empire. For those who could afford a house, whether in Rome or outside the city, furnishings were usually sparse. One might find beds with mattresses of fine-combed wool set on wooden slats or ropes, a cupboard,

102. FIGURAL MOSAIC
Perhaps from Utica, Tunisia
First half of 3rd c. AD
L. 205.5 cm.
MS 4012

An intriguing puzzle, this mosaic appears to be an adaptation of a now lost mosaic from Hadrumentum (Sousse). It probably came from the Roman Tunisian town of Utica and represents Theseus sailing away from the Cretan labyrinth, here mostly missing. Its inscription, VINCLVSVS, repeated twice, remains controversial.

103. TERRACOTTA LAMPS

1st–2nd centuries AD
L. 11 cm MS 2117
L. 10 cm MS 314

The lamps depict a running warrior and a racing chariot.

and small tables in a bedroom. Couches, chairs, and small tables furnished the dining and sitting rooms. Ordinary furniture was made of wood. More extravagant versions were made of marble, wood, and bronze or with inlay.

The walls of Roman interiors were normally coated with successive layers of plaster. The top layer contained alabaster or marble dust that could take a high sheen. A range of pigments was available for imitating colored marble or painting elaborate pictorial scenes. Sometimes the houses and villas of the wealthy had more elaborate wall decoration of inlaid colored marbles or glass plaques.

Mosaic flooring, the decorative equivalent of carpeting, was in near universal use throughout the Roman Empire. In the 3rd–2nd century BC this art form was modified through the use of *tesserae*—cubes of stone, glass, or glazed terracotta cut to uniform sizes. Tessellated mosaics became the norm in the Roman period.

Lighting, Plumbing, and Heating

Oil-burning lamps were the primary source for artificial light in Roman houses. Cheap lamps were made mold-made terracotta, more expensive ones of bronze or even gold. The upper circular surface of the lamp, the discus, bore decorative images. Lamp stands for multiple hanging or resting lamps would have been essential for lighting larger rooms. Because the olive oil used for fuel was expensive, however, a household on a tight budget would have tried to use lamps judiciously.

Until well into the 19th century, there was no more sophisticated water supply system in the world than that of the Roman Empire. City water was carried overland by a system of aqueducts to large cisterns or reservoirs. A wealthy Roman had water piped directly to the house. Most private citizens, however, drew their water from the public fountain house. Every Roman town had *thermae* (public

DID ROMAN WATER PIPES CAUSE LEAD POISONING?

Much of the water supply of Rome and other cities throughout the empire traveled through lead pipes carried by aqueducts. Many inhabitants of Rome dined on lead tableware and drank wine made in lead vessels. Did they suffer from lead poisoning?

Much unsubstantiated speculation surrounds this question. The ancient texts are silent. Archaeologists have found quantities of lead in ancient Roman soils, but only traces of lead have been detected in a small number of ancient Roman skeletons. At present, the question of lead poisoning (and its implications) remains unresolved.

104. INSCRIBED LEAD WATER PIPE
Probably from Rome, AD 69–79
L. 37.5 cm
L-1033-60
Stamp: ...ALOAVGVESPASIANI
SVBCVRACALLISIIAVGL PROG

The stamp dates the pipe to the reign of the emperor Vespasian. This pipe, or one like it, carried water from the reservoirs of Rome to private houses or public buildings. In its original state, it may have been ten feet long and weighed over 500 pounds.

On loan from the Department of Classical Studies and Ancient History, University of Pennsylvania.

105. Hypocaust heating system in the Trajanic baths at Cyrene, North Africa. This ingenious Roman system of heating rooms used stacks of clay disks or bricks. Arranged in a checkerboard pattern beneath the floor, they retained and circulated hot air generated from a nearby furnace.

Courtesy of D. White.

bathing establishments). Men and women had separate accommodations.

An ordinary Roman house was heated mainly by portable coal-burning braziers. In the early 1st century BC the Romans invented the *suspensura*, a hollow floor with a hypocaust heating system. Thereafter, wealthy Roman houses and public baths were outfitted with flues and vents for the circulation of warm air, especially in the northern regions.

Dining in the Roman House

According to ancient authors, Romans of the Imperial period normally ate three meals a day: *ientaculum*, a light breakfast of bread, cheese, and fruit after sunrise; *prandium*, a midday lunch of eggs, fish, cold meats, vegetables, and bread; and, in the evening, *cena*, the main meal of the day.

The eating habits of the Romans varied from region to region and from class to class. Just as in our culture, Roman households established their own dining schedules and menus. By the time of the Roman Empire a great variety of foods were available to the prosperous Roman citizen.

Cena for an ancient Roman could have been a simple meal or a grand banquet. It was served in the *triclinium*, or dining room. Men and women both dined in the reclining position, propped on cushions, while children sat on stools beside the couches. Dining utensils included knives, toothpicks, and spoons. The fork had not yet been invented and eating with one's hands was expected! Slaves brought around towels and water

106. MODERN BRONZE REPLICA OF A SILENUS STATUETTE

Original from Pompeii, 1st century AD
H. 39 cm
MS 3688

Amusing statuettes such as this one of Selinus riding on his wineskin were used as decorative table items in wealthy Roman houses. Although the bronze is heavy the hollow wineskin almost certainly served as a wine decanter. The statuette was cast in the late 19th century from an original in the Naples Museum.

MENU FROM TRIMALCHIO'S FEAST

Trimalchio's orgy, described by Petronius in his satirical work, *The Satyricon* (1st century AD), included the following menu:

Gustatio (appetizers), served with honeyed wine
 White and black olives
 Dormice (sweets) sprinkled with honey and poppy seeds
 Grilled sausages
 Plums and pomegranate seeds
 Beccaficos (small birds) in spiced egg yolk

Fercula (main courses), served with 100-year old Falerian wine
 Foods of the Zodiac served on a round plate marked with the signs: chick-peas (the
  sign of Aries); beef (Taurus); kidneys (Gemini); crown of myrtle (Cancer);
  African figs (Leo); sterile sow's womb (Virgo); scales supporting tarts and honey
  cakes (Libra); scorpion fish (Scorpio); eyefish (Sagittarius); lobster (Capricorn);
  goose (Aquarius); two red mullets (Pisces)
 Roasted fattened fowls, sow bellies, and hare
 Roast whole wild boar with dates, suckled by piglets made of cakes and stuffed with live
  thrushes
 Boiled whole pig stuffed with sausage and black puddings

Mensa secunda (dessert)
 Fruits and cakes
 Boned, fattened chickens and goose eggs
 Pastry thrushes stuffed with raisins and nuts
 Quince apples and pork disguised as fowls and fish
 Oysters and scallops
 Snails

107. BLACK-GLOSS DINING VESSELS

LEFT: ECHINUS BOWL
Ca. 3rd century BC
Diam. 14.5 cm
MS 5774

BOTTOM: PLATE
Possibly from Pompeii or the
vicinity, early 3rd century BC
Diam. 23.8 cm
65-39-1

RIGHT: SHALLOW BOWL
Minturnae, Italy, in a refuse heap
from a potter's shop, 3rd–2nd
centuries BC
Diam. 15.3 cm
32-36-28

bowls for washing hands between courses. The wealthy dined on vessels of silver and gold, while the average citizen might have had a set of glass plates, bowls, and cups for special occasions and ceramic dishes for everyday use.

Roman Tableware

The average Roman household used ceramic dishes for everyday meals. The fine ceramic wares used by the Romans in the 3rd through early 1st centuries BC were black-gloss vessels of the type long manufactured by the Greeks. This Republican period black-gloss pottery was made in several areas, including Etruria.

A Roman preference for red-slipped or red-gloss tableware originated in the eastern Mediterranean around 150 BC and appeared in Italy in the 1st century BC. They were used throughout the Imperial period as the

108. RED-GLOSS TABLEWARES

TOP: RED-GLOSS HEMISPHERI-
CAL BOWL

Made in Rome or central Italy, late
1st–early 2nd centuries AD
Diam. 11 cm
31-36-21

The vessel at the top bears the
potter's stamp OCT.PRO, an abbreviation for L. Octavius Proclus,
within the form of a foot.

RIGHT: EASTERN SIGILLATA A
BOWL

Beth Shean, Israel, North Cemetery
Tomb 206, ca. AD 10–60/70
Diam 8.7 cm
29-102-546

LEFT: EASTERN SIGILLATA A
BOWL

Beth Shean, Israel, North Cemetery
Tomb 206, ca. AD 50–75
Diam. 10.3 cm
29-102-549

CENTER: EASTERN SIGILLATA B
SALT CELLAR

Beth Shean, Israel. Made in western
Anatolia, AD 50–80
Diam. 4.5 cm
29-102-547

common tableware of the Romans. Much of this fine red ware was elaborately decorated with stamps. Thus another common term for these wares is *terra sigillata*, "stamped clay."

Dining service for the wealthy was of precious silver and gold. However, only rare examples have survived from antiquity. Bronze wares were a more modest option for the average household, and could be gilded to imitate the more precious wares.

With the introduction of glass blowing in the 1st century BC, glass manufacturing grew into a booming industry. For the first time, simple glass vessels became affordable to the average Roman family. Extravagant, specially commissioned pieces attracted the wealthy consumer.

109. GLASS SPICE JAR
Beth Shean, Israel, 4th century AD
Diam. 9 cm
MS 4933A

110. GLASS SQUAT JUG
Probably from Aleppo, Syria, 4th century AD
H. 12.8 cm
MS 5134

111. GLASS STEM-FOOTED WINE CUP
Syria-Palestine, 3rd century AD
H. 7.6 cm
MS 5121

112. MARBLE PORTRAIT OF A MIDDLE-AGED WOMAN

Probably from Sardinia,
ca. AD 10–20
H. 36 cm
MS 4919

The Roman ideal of the modest woman with strength of character is expressed clearly in this powerful, individualized portrait of an unidentified female. The close dating of the sculpture comes from a comparison of the hair style with that on representations of Livia and Julia, the wife and daughter of Augustus.

Women in Roman Society

Romans of the Republican and Imperial periods maintained a conservative ideal of womanhood. This ideal included loyalty to the family, a personal austerity and modesty in habits and lifestyle, civic responsibility, and generosity.

By law Roman women were subject to male guardians throughout their lives, as daughters, granddaughters, sisters, or wives. Roman women were not granted the right to participate in civic or political matters until the edict of AD 212 made every freed slave a full Roman citizen. Throughout the Roman Empire, however, women from the elite classes of society did indeed exercise significant political power. This was particularly true for members of the imperial family. Even Roman women outside the ruling classes sometimes achieved considerable financial independence and used that independence for the civic good and for political ends. Within the home most Roman women exercised power and a degree of autonomy.

Roman women of all classes took part in religious activities, though the majority of the cults were dominated by men. Mystery cults, such as the cult of the Egyptian goddess Isis, were particularly attractive to women, who were given roles as priestesses. The rituals themselves offered some degree of excitement and escape from a woman's everyday life.

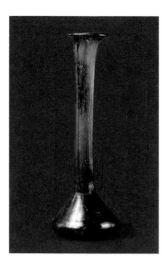

113. GLASS *UNGUENTARIUM*
Probably from Luxor, Egypt,
2nd century AD
H 14.7 cm
MS 5518

Perfume and Cosmetics

Well-to-do Romans, both men and women, used perfumes daily and lavishly. The Roman perfume industry, however, was secondary to the manufacture of oil, the base for perfumed unguents.

The most common unguents of that period were olive oil, myrtle oil, and mastic scented with roses, lavender, saffron, marjoram, crushed henna, and pomegranate rind. The most expensive perfumes used exotic ingredients imported from the Orient.

Romans also had a love for cosmetics. The well-to-do Roman lady employed an *ornatrix*, a female servant who was both a hairdresser and a make-up artist. A properly made-up

115. GLASS DOUBLE VESSEL
Probably from Beth Jibrin, Israel,
late 4th–5th centuries AD
H. 8 cm
MS 5237A, B

Vessels of this type were used to hold black eye makeup, called galena, in one compartment and bronze applicators in the other, as seen here.

114. GLASS FLASK
Probably from Yebna, Syria, late
2nd–3rd centuries AD
H. 12.6 cm
MS 5114

116. GLASS DOUBLE VESSEL
5th century AD
H. 26.9 cm
86-35-53

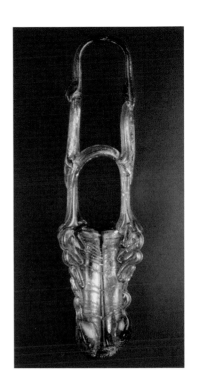

Roman matron would have had a *capsa* (make-up kit) with *unguentaria* (glass ointment bottles) containing henna for hair coloring, chalk and white lead to whiten her skin, ochre or the lees of wine to redden her cheeks, and kohl, ashes, or powdered galena (lead sulphide) to blacken her eyebrows and eyelids.

Roman Jewelry

During the Roman Republic the state took a conservative approach to the wearing of jewelry, placing limits on the amount of gold a woman could wear. By the Roman Imperial period, however, there were few restrictions on the wearing and ownership of jewelry. Gold jewelry was greatly prized, and the purity of the gold almost never dipped below 18 carats (about 75% pure gold). Silver jewelry, which corrodes, has not survived in great quantities from the Roman period.

Romans were fond of incorporating brightly colored precious and semiprecious gemstones in their jewelry, especially carnelians, garnets, Egyptian emeralds, Ceylonese sapphires, cit-

117. GOLD EARRINGS
Made in the eastern Roman Empire,
3rd century AD
H. 5 cm
58-9-2A, B

118. BANDED GLASS PASTE GEM FROM RING SETTING
Late 1st century BC
H. 2.1 cm
29-128-1846

Queen Omphale, the seductress of Hercules, appears with his attributes, the lion skin and club.

**119. NECKLACE
WITH GLASS EYE
BEADS**
Karanog, Nubia, Grave
712, Roman Imperial period
L. 36 cm
E 7920

rines, peridots, amethysts, and, in rare instances, uncut diamond crystals. Freshwater pearls from the Persian Gulf were extremely popular. Glass was a staple of less expensive Roman jewelry. Glass inlay, glass beads imitating precious stones, and solid glass bangles were common.

In the Roman Imperial period finger rings were worn by both men and women. They were used as seals for documents, marriage rings, good luck charms, badges of one's class (for example as a senator or equestrian}, and purely as decoration.

Roman Children

The day-to-day raising and educating of Roman children were the prime responsibilities of the mother. For the lower classes this meant seeing that children were prepared for their life's work. Girls learned how to run a household, cook, clean, sew, embroider, and weave. Boys learned the father's occupation or apprenticed at a young age in a trade.

Educated upper-class women taught their children the basics of reading and writing Latin and Greek. A nurse or a *pedagogue* (a slave who served as tutor and servant) might also be employed. Roman girls might be married as early as 12 or 13 years of age. Their level of education depended on the mother's ability and interest in teaching or the family's ability to hire a tutor.

Boys of middle- and upper-class families were sent to private elementary schools where they were taught reading, writing, and arithmetic. After their primary education, boys might study with a more advanced teacher who could teach the core subjects of Latin literature, Greek literature and rhetoric, and perhaps geography, history, science, music, and mathematics.

We know very little about Roman children and their daily activities, however. From the archaeological remains of games and toys we can suppose that there were leisure times when household chores were done and children were free to enjoy themselves.

120. MUMMY PORTRAIT OF TEKOSIS

Tempera on cedarwood panels
Probably from near Assyut, Egypt, ca. AD 180–200
L. 33 cm
L-2000-2.21

Tekosis, daughter of Harunis, appears to be a girl of around 11 or 12 years of age who died before marriage. The white veil may signify the marital status she never achieved, while the flat silver neckband is like those worn by children on other mummy portraits.

On loan from the Department of Classics, Swarthmore College.

121. MARBLE PORTRAIT OF THE BOY CALIGULA (?)

Early 1st century AD
H. 20 cm
MS 4030

This head bears a striking resemblance to representations of the boy Caligula. Modelling private funerary portraits of children after members of the imperial family was common. Thus this could as well portray an unidentified boy, done in the guise of a Julio-Claudian prince.

122. Hadrian's Mausoleum (Castel Sant'Angelo), Rome. This colossal tomb was built for the emperor Hadrian (AD 117–138), his family, and his successors. It originally rose even higher than it does today and was topped with an earth mound. It served as a fortress for the popes during the Middle Ages and remains to this day one of Rome's most conspicuous monuments.

Courtesy of I. B. Romano.

DEATH AND BURIAL

Roman funerary practices shifted between burning the bodies of the dead (cremation) and burying them intact (inhumation). Graves varied from simple tile-lined holes in the ground to extravagant above-ground monuments rising several storeys high.

For health reasons and out of fear of the spirits of the dead, Romans usually set their cemeteries along roads outside the city limits. These were carefully landscaped and sometimes even provided with gardens. The great underground Jewish and Christian catacombs, created in the 2nd and 3rd centuries AD on the outskirts of Roman cities, evolved into virtual multi-leveled cities of the dead.

The Roman cult of the dead called for a highly elaborate set of rituals. These began with a funeral, which lasted from the moment of death until the final burial ceremony. In the years following the burial, additional rites were carried out either at the grave site or nearby to honor the memory of the deceased.

Roman Tombs

The inscriptions and sculptural decorations applied to the exteriors of above-ground Roman tombs usually hark back to the life and achievements of the dead, but they can also symbolize what the deceased hoped would

123. MARBLE GRAVE RELIEF

Athens, ca. AD 150
H. 64 cm
63-6-1

The deceased lady is shown in full frontal view. She wears a low *polos* head-dress. It is likely that she has been initiated into the rites of Demeter/ Ceres whose cult promised its followers a life after death. The originally inscribed pediment and much of the frame are now missing.

lie ahead for them for the rest of eternity. The facades of Roman tombs incorporate a wide range of styles, designs, and materials that reflect the breadth and cultural diversity of the Roman world. The final resting places of the very wealthy achieved enormous size and magnificence. The burial places of the emperors and members of the imperial family surpassed even these.

The Romans, like the Etruscans before them, believed that tombs should recall the world of the living. Depending on their shape and size, tomb interiors could mirror the interiors of houses and even palaces of the living. Richly carved sarcophagi (stone coffins) were positioned so that they could be seen. Such tombs were clearly intended to be visited by generations of the living.

124. MARBLE *ELOGIUM*
Rome or vicinity, 1st–2nd centuries AD
L. 30 cm
L-1033-58
C. CATILIVS C. L. PRIMVS
CATILIA C. L. PRIMA

"Gaius Catilius Primus, freedman of Gaius (Catilius); Catilia Prima, freed-woman of Gaius (Catilius)" The abbreviation C. L. stands for *Gaius libertus* (Gaius the freedman) and indicates the dead couple's relationship to their former master.

On loan from the Department of Classical Studies and Ancient History, University of Pennsylvania.

Tombstones and Inscriptions

Sculpted stone reliefs attached to Roman tombs cover a wide range of themes, from portrayals of the dead to scenes glorifying their past achievements, everyday lives, or aspects of the life to come. Like contemporary tombstones, they sometimes carry epitaphs relating to the deceased.

Plain funeral *elogia* (epitaphic inscriptions) are more explicitly Roman. Most were attached to the tomb wall or under the niche that held either the dead person's bust or their ash urn. Some refer to freedmen or freed-women, ex-slaves who had adopted the *praenomen* (first name) and the *nomen* (clan name) of their owners after receiving their freedom. Others are dedicated to the "Shades of the Dead," the departed ancestors of the deceased.

Inhumation Burials

Only a few full-size carved coffins survive from Republican Rome (509–31 BC), a time when burning the bodies of the dead (cremation) was preferred to burying them intact (inhumation). The great period of coffin use began in the early 2nd century AD, when inhumation became the prevailing rite.

Sculpted marble sarcophagi (stone coffins), manufactured either in Athens

125. LIMESTONE *LOCULUS* COVER

Palmyra, Syria, 2nd century AD
H. 50 cm
CBS 8904

This bust of a woman of high status, perhaps a priestess, is adorned with an elaborate headdress and jewelry. Palmyra's inhabitants spoke Aramaic and Greek in the 2nd century AD, when this cover was carved. The "Aramaic" epitaph here is false, however. It was added in modern times in an attempt to increase its market value.

126. LIMESTONE *LOCULUS* COVER

Palmyra, Syria, 2nd century AD
H. 50 cm
CBS 8902

The sculpted covers that seal the *loculi* in Palmyra's Valley of the Dead provide considerable information about Palmyrene burial customs, religion, and local life. This
cover depicts a youth reclining with a vase in his left hand. Two males in smaller
scale, perhaps slaves, stand by, holding an amphora and a cup. Their rigidly frontal
poses and stiff figural style are hallmarks of the provincial Roman style in Syria.

127. MARBLE *LOCULUS* COVER

Late 2nd–3rd centuries AD
L. 175.6 cm
MS 4017

The scene represents a Bacchic procession, with the triumphant god Bacchus at the left in a
low chariot drawn by an old centaur. The women with dresses billowing over their heads are
the god's companions, called maenads. The others are satyrs, little Eros figures, and the god's
sacred animals, the panther and the lion. The right-hand third of the cover is a restoration.

128. GLASS CINERARY URN

Late 1st century AD
H. 21.4 cm
MS 5553A, B

Originally made to store food, this bulky jar was later recycled as a cinerary urn. Because of its fragility it needed a terracotta or lead outer liner. Its hollow lid was drilled to work as a funnel. When inverted the lid directed the flow of wine or perfumed oil over the ashes.

and Asia Minor or in the west, were traded throughout the Roman world until the end of the 3rd century AD. The exports from Athens were often shipped rough-finished and their final carving completed locally to the specifications of the deceased's survivors. Inexpensive wooden coffins seldom survive but must have been widely used by the poor, as were terracotta coffins.

Sometimes the dead were placed in niches or compartments within tombs. These *loculi* were then sealed with stone covers, often elaborately carved.

Cremation Burials

Although cremation and inhumation practices had coexisted in Rome since the Iron Age (8th to 6th centuries BC), by the time of the Republic and Early Imperial years (400 BC–AD 100) cremation became the more typical way to dispose of bodies (for those who could afford the price of fuelwood). Cremation became rare by the early 2nd century AD and was largely driven out of use in the 4th century by the Christian belief in the resurrection of the body.

129. SEATED GOD WITH A LION

Roman Imperial period with restorations in Italy in the early 17th century or before
H. with plinth, 137 cm
MS 5483

To judge by his youthful and idealized appearance, the panther skin draped over the rocky seat, and the lion, the seated figure is probably Dionysos. The statue group was originally meant to be seen in the round and was probably a decorative piece for a Roman garden or villa. Sometime later, holes were cut through the neck of the lion and the back of Dionysos to create a fountain sculpture. The head of Dionysos, the muzzle of the lion, and fragments of the toes and fingers are restorations probably added in the 15th to early 17th centuries in Italy. The statue was purchased by the University of Pennsylvania Museum from a dealer in 1911 and has a pedigree that goes back to 1622. It illustrates how over the centuries interest in the classical world has waxed and waned, yet endures.

4

The Legacy of Ancient Classical Civilizations

The legacy of the ancient Greeks, Etruscans, and Romans is so much a part of western culture and daily life that we tend to forget the specific debt we owe to the past. Classical literature and mythology and classical art forms and themes have enriched our culture immeasurably. Our democratic form of government, the languages we speak, the alphabet we use, and the very pennies we save are all part of our heritage from the past.

The classically educated founding fathers of the American Republic were well versed in the democratic ideals of Greece and the governmental structure of the Roman Republic. They drew on both classical example and European models to plan their own young government. These included the concept of two legislative bodies, the notion of checks and balances, and the process of impeachment. Much of the symbolism and visual imagery of the new democracy drew directly on ancient Greece and Rome.

The Greek and Latin languages are woven into most of the modern European languages. In the English language the use of Latin expressions or derivatives is pervasive in technical fields and in everyday speech. The Etruscans gave many words to the Romans, who Latinized them. Some of these passed on to English. The English alphabet goes directly back to the ancient Greeks and Romans. The very word *alphabet* is Greek and is taken from the first two letters of the Greek alphabet, alpha and beta. The Greeks borrowed the alphabetic system from the Phoenicians around 800 BC. The Etruscans transmitted the Greek alphabet to the Romans, who added lower case letters around 300 AD.

Modern coinage can also be traced directly back to the Greeks and Romans. Scholars ascribe its invention to the Greeks of western Asia Minor or their Lydian neighbors sometime around 600 BC. No longer did merchants and consumers have to use the barter system or weigh out lumps of metal bullion in order to make a purchase.

Alexander the Great spread Greek culture thousands of miles east, as far as India. The influence of the Roman Empire was vast. But today's world is wider and more varied than even the most cosmopolitan citizen of Rome could have envisioned. The legacy of the classical past joins with other great heritages in shaping the modern world.

Suggested Reading

Readers who would like to continue their exploration of the Etruscan and Roman worlds may find the following publications to be helpful.

THE ETRUSCAN WORLD

Bonfante, Larissa. *Reading the Past: Etruscan.* Berkeley: University of California Press, 1990.

Bonfante, Larissa, ed. *Etruscan Life and Afterlife: A Handbook of Etruscan Studies.* Detroit: Wayne State University Press, 1986.

Brendel, Otto J. *Etruscan Art.* 2nd ed. Pelican History of Art. New Haven, CT: Yale University Press, 1995.

Haynes, Sybille. *Etruscan Civilization: A Cultural History.* Malibu: Getty Publications, 2000.

Macnamara, Ellen. *The Etruscans.* Cambridge, MA: Harvard University Press, 1991.

THE ROMAN WORLD

Carcopino, Jerome. *Daily Life in Ancient Rome: The People and the City at the Height of the Empire.* New Haven, CT: Yale University Press, 1940.

Henig, Martin, ed. *A Handbook of Roman Art.* Ithaca, NY: Cornell University Press, 1983.

MacKendrick, Paul. *Mute Stones Speak: The Story of Archaeology in Italy.* New York: St. Martin's Press, 1960.

Ramage, Nancy H., and Andrew Ramage. *Roman Art: Romulus to Constantine.* Englewood Cliffs, NJ: Prentice Hall, 1996.

Scarre, Chris. *Chronicle of the Roman Emperors.* New York: Thames and Hudson, 1995.

RECENT PUBLICATIONS ON THE ETRUSCAN AND ROMAN COLLECTIONS OF THE UNIVERSITY OF PENNSYLVANIA MUSEUM

Berges, Dietrich. "Hidden Treasures from the Vault: Engraved Gems from the Maxwell Sommerville Collection." *Expedition* 41, no. 1 (1999): 17–28.

Bilde, Pia Guldager. "Those Nemi Sculptures…: Marbles from a

Roman Sanctuary in the University of Pennsylvania Museum." *Expedition* 40, no. 3 (1998): 34–47.

Fleming, Stuart J. *Roman Glass: Reflections on Cultural Change.* Philadelphia: University of Pennsylvania Museum of Archaeology and Anthropology, 1999.

_____. *Roman Glass: Reflections of Everyday Life.* Philadelphia: University of Pennsylvania Museum of Archaeology and Anthropology, 1997.

_____, issue ed. "Glass in the Roman World." *Expedition* 38, no.2 (1996): 1–64.

Flower, Harriet I. "A Tale of Two Monuments: Domitian, Trajan, and Some Praetorians at Puteoli (AE 1973, 137)." *American Journal of Archaeology* 105 (2001): 625–48.

Livi, Valentina. "A Story Told in Pieces: Architectural Terracottas from Minturnae, Italy." *Expedition* 44, no. 1 (2002): 24–35.

Ridgway, Brunilde Sismondo. "Is the Hope Head an Italian Goddess? A Case of Circumstantial Evidence." *Expedition* 38, no. 3 (1996): 55–62.

Warden, P. Gregory. *The Hilprecht Collection of Greek, Italic and Roman Bronzes in the University of Pennsylvania Museum.* Philadelphia: The University Museum, University of Pennsylvania, 1997.

White, Donald. "Of Coffins, Curses, and Other Plumbeous Matters: The Museum's Lead Burial Casket from Tyre." *Expedition* 39, no. 3 (1997): 3–14.

White, Donald, Keith DeVries, David G. Romano, Irene Bald Romano, and Yelena Stolyarik. *The Ancient Greek World: The Rodney S. Young Gallery.* Philadelphia: University of Pennsylvania Museum, 1995.

About the Authors

DR. DONALD WHITE, Curator-in-Charge of the Mediterranean Section since 1990, is the head curator of the new Etruscan and Roman Galleries. Dr. White has been a Curator in the Mediterranean Section and a Professor of Classical Archaeology since 1974. He has taught at Princeton University and the University of Michigan and has held honorary appointments at Oxford University and Harvard University. Dr. White has conducted archaeological field research at Morgantina, Sicily, at Apollonia and Cyrene in Libya, and at Marsa Matruh, Egypt. He is the author of three major books, two of them on his excavations at the Sanctuary of Demeter and Persephone at Cyrene, and over seventy articles and reviews. He was the curator of "The Ancient Greek World" exhibition at the University Museum.

DR. ANN BLAIR BROWNLEE, Senior Research Scientist in the Mediterranean Section, is the co-curator of the Etruscan and Roman Galleries. Dr. Brownlee is an Adjunct Assistant Professor in the History of Art Department at the University of Pennsylvania, and has taught at Rutgers University and Lehigh University. She received her Ph.D. from Harvard University in 1981, and has participated in archaeological field research at various sites on Cyprus and at Corinth in Greece. She is the author of numerous articles and a forthcoming book on Greek vase painting and is a specialist on relations between the Greeks and Etruscans. She is co-director of the University Museum's *Corpus Vasorum Antiquorum* project and the author of the series' volumes on Attic black-figured vases.

DR. IRENE BALD ROMANO, Research Associate of the Mediterranean Section, is the co-curator and coordinator of the Etruscan and Roman Galleries. Dr. Romano has been affiliated with the University Museum since 1980 in a variety of capacities, including Registrar, Coordinator of Exhibits and Collections, and Consulting Scholar for the "Ancient Greek World" exhibition. She is a specialist in Greek and Roman sculpture, terracotta figurines, and Hellenistic pottery, and has published numerous articles and two books on these topics. Dr. Romano received her Ph.D. from the University of Pennsylvania in 1980 and has taught at the University of Pennsylvania and at Franklin and Marshall College. She has participated in archaeological field research in Spain, Greece, Turkey, and Italy, including most recently at the excavations at a Roman villa site on the shores of Lake Nemi.

DR. JEAN MACINTOSH TURFA, Curatorial Consultant for the Etruscan Collections and Exhibition, teaches Etruscan art and archaeology at Bryn Mawr College. She received her Ph.D. in 1974 from Bryn Mawr College and has participated in archaeological field research in the U.S., U.K., Greece, and Italy. Dr. Turfa has also taught at the University of Illinois, Chicago Circle, at Loyola University of Chicago, the University of Liverpool, and at the University of Manchester. She has published numerous articles on Etruscan art and archaeology, on the relationships between the Etruscans and their neighbors, and on Etruscan trade.

Concordance of Object Numbers and Illustrations

Object no.	Illustration	Object no.	Illustration	Object no.	Illustration
29-100-5	96	L-29-47	40	MS 2511	55
29-102-544	96	L-51-1	66	MS 2517	54
29-102-546	108	L-64-478	48	MS 2520	32
29-102-547	108	L-64-539	38	MS 2734	22
29-102-549	108	L-64-551	48	MS 2732A, B	31
29-108-105	100	L-64-553	48	MS 2751	15
29-126-601	91	L-1033-58	124	MS 3200	35
29-126-626	91	L-1033-60	104	MS 3344A, B	23
29-126-781	91	L-2000-2.21	120	MS 3345A–C	34
29-126-823A	91	MS 215	74	MS 3350	42
29-126-873A	90	MS 310	23	MS 3444	46
29-126-888	61	MS 314	103	MS 3448	82
29-126-935	92	MS 560A	37	MS 3453	81
29-126-937	62	MS 642	39	MS 3459	84
29-126-949	92	MS 714	28	MS 3465	83
29-126-960	92	MS 761	21	MS 3483	80
29-126-965	63	MS 787A–C	20	MS 3488	58
29-126-1049	64	MS 850	17	MS 3496	47
29-126-1087	92	MS 851	18	MS 3688	106
29-126-1103	93	MS 853	19	MS 4012	102
29-126-1138	93	MS 1044	13	MS 4017	127
29-126-1178	65	MS 1137B	12	MS 4018	75
29-128-542	24	MS 1155	12	MS 4021	33
29-128-900	76	MS 1221–1222	14	MS 4030	121
29-128-1846	118	MS 1284	44	MS 4096	96
31-36-21	108	MS 1355–1363	29	MS 4877A	96
32-36-3	88	MS 1407-1423	77	MS 4916	67
32-36-28	107	MS 1425-1427	77	MS 4916	68
32-36-64	86	MS 1428	59	MS 4917	70
32-36-66	87	MS 1506	57	MS 4919	112
48-2-103	78	MS 1519	11	MS 4933A	109
48-2-223	72	MS 1525	25	MS 4980	97
48-2-268	73	MS 1598	9	MS 4990	97
48-2-271	71	MS 1601	10	MS 4993	97
54-3-1	69	MS 1606	26	MS 5114	97
57-3-1A, B	36	MS 1609	45	MS 5114	114
58-9-2A, B	117	MS 1630	48	MS 5121	111
59-24-1	43	MS 1637	27	MS 5134	110
63-6-1	123	MS 1801	Frontispiece	MS 5237A, B	115
65-39-1	107	MS 1803	52	MS 5483	129
86-35-53	116	MS 1804	51	MS 5518	113
86-35-82	97	MS 1806	53	MS 5553A, B	128
89-2-3	94	MS 1830	49	MS 5656A	101
89-2-4	95	MS 1832	50	MS 5697	30
CBS 8902	126	MS 2117	103	MS 5752	48
CBS 8904	125	MS 2152	98	MS 5756	48
E 7920	119	MS 2314	41	MS 5757	48
E 12952	93	MS 2458A, B	56	MS 5774	107

Index

bold indicates illustration numbers

mythological creatures
    Medusa **36, 101**
    faun **83**
    satyr **84**
    Silenus **106**
mythology 55, 65
Oriental and Egyptianizing cults 49
priests **74**
rituals 82
sanctuaries 51
temples 51
votives 51, 55, **77, 78, 81**
replicas 3, 4, **3**
Roman Britain 68
Roman coin collections 6
    Beth Shean, Israel 6
    Brock gift 6
    Leptis Magna excavations 7
    Memphis, Egypt, excavations 6
    Meydum, Egypt 6
    Minturnae, Italy 7
Roman colonies, colonial cities 57, 59
    Colonia Minturnae. *See* Minturnae
    North African provinces 59, 65, 68, **89**
Roman commerce and trade 56, 64–67, 83
    brick trade 67
        brickstamps 67, **98**
    crafts tradition 57, 66
        workshops 66
    manufacturing 59, 67, 75, 84
        oil 78
    maritime trade 64
Roman daily life 68
    bathing 72
        thermae (public baths) 70–71, **70, 105**
    children's lives 69, 72, 80, **120**
        apprenticeships 80
        boys 80, **121**
        education 80
        girls 80, **120**
        leisure time 80
    dining 72, 74, 75
        triclinium (dining room) 72
        utensils and tableware 66, 72, 74, 75,
            96, 106–108, 110, 111
        variety of foods 72
    elite classes 69, 72, 74, 75, 77, 80
    freedmen, freedwomen 66, 84
    marriage 77, 80
    travel 59
    women's lives 55, 69, 72, 77, 78, 79, 80
        children 80
        cosmetics 78
        financial independence 77

guardianship of 77
jewelry 79, 80
marriage 80
priestesses 77
servants 78
Roman emperors 42
    "Adoptive" Emperors 43
    Aemilianus **92**
    Alexander Severus 43
    Antoninus Pius 43
    Augustus (Octavius) 41, 42, 82, 49, 57, **61**
    Aurelian 43, 60, **93**
    Caligula 42, **121**
    Claudius 42
    Commodus and the Severans 43
    Constantine the Great 44, 50, **65**
    Constantius II **66**
    Didius Julianus 43
    Diocletian 44, 60, **93**
    Domitian 43, 45, **68, 92**
    Flavians 43
    Hadrian 43, **63, 122**
    Julio-Claudian 42
    Marcus Aurelius 43
    Maximianus **93**
    Nero 42, 60
    Otho **92**
    Septimius Severus 43, **64**
    Titus 43
    Tiberius 42
    Trajan 43, 45, **68, 92**
    Vespasian 43, **62**
Roman empire 41, 44, 59, 72, 77
    demise of 41
Roman glass collections 7
Roman gods. *See* religion
Roman government 41, 42, 89
    imperial 42
    republican 41, 42, 57, 89
        consuls 42
    Senate 42, 43, 45, **129**
    state subsidies 59
Roman military 43, 45
    legions 43, **67**
    outposts 57
    soldiers 45, **68, 69, 76**
Roman provinces in Africa 59, 65, 68, **89, 105**
Rome 41, 49, 57, 67, 68, 69, 84, 87, **60, 72, 75,**
    93, 101, 104, 108, 122, 124, 129
    Forum **60**

Samos, Greece 29
Sanctuary of Diana Nemorensis 4, 54–55, **3,**
    5, 79–84

UNIVERSITY OF MICHIGAN

3 9015 08074 0049